# Praise fc

"Solid! Bill gives not only a biblical basis for our 'greater work' but a proven pathway to consistently live as a multiplying disciple of Jesus. I am a better disciple maker because of knowing Bill Wilks and reading this book."

**—Dr. Scott E. Sullivan**
**Discipleship Catalyst and SPARK Conference Director**
**Georgia Baptist Mission Board**

"Bill has a passion to make disciples through the local church. This book is a reflection of the greatest work before us as we strive to make disciples. He outlines for us an easy path to a lifestyle of discipleship. He even made me remember my first Zebco 33."

**—Dr. Jody Dean**
**Associate Professor of Christian Education**
**New Orleans Baptist Theological Seminary**

"In the days when competition for our attention grows fiercer, Bill Wilks cut through the static to deliver what we need. *The Greater Work* is a clear and accessible call that will inspire and equip you as a disciple-making force for God's work in the world. Read this book, accept its challenge, and go change the world by God's grace."

**—Dr. Philip Nation**
**Vice President and Publisher**
**Thomas Nelson Bibles**

"As the concept of disciple-making has found renewed vigor and interest among church families in recent days, church leaders and individual believers are interested in learning exactly what this means and how to embrace a lifestyle of discipleship amid all that is happening around us. If you are ready to move from thinking about a lifestyle of disciple-making to embracing it as a reality, then you'll want to read Bill Wilks's book *The Greater Work*. Bill shares about real people discovering their own path, how to apply biblical concepts in a simple and straightforward manner, and why it's important to be intentional in our effort. As he outlines specific steps to get started, you'll feel like Bill is sitting across the table walking you through the process, and by the time you finish the book, you'll have the tools and confidence you need to live the D-Life."

—**Jennifer Davis Rash**
**President and Editor-in-Chief**
**The Alabama Baptist Newspaper**

# THE GREATER WORK

## DISCIPLE-MAKING. ANYTIME. ANYWHERE.

BILL WILKS

līfe™
Bible Study

Birmingham, Alabama

Life Bible Study
100 Missionary Ridge
Birmingham, AL 35242
Life Bible Study is an imprint of Iron Stream Media
LifeBibleStudy.com
IronStreamMedia.com

Library of Congress Control Number: 2021944826

ISBN: 978-1-63204-119-7 paperback
ISBN: 978-1-63204-120-3 ebook

1 2 3 4 5—26 25 24 23 22
Printed in the United States of America

# Dedication

I dedicate *The Greater Work* to my two incredible grandchildren, Livingston and Roman. I pray that God will use this book to fan the flames of a disciple-making movement that will help us reach your generation and see God's Kingdom advance on earth. Pop wants to make the world a better place for you. I love you both more than life.

I also dedicate it to my dear brother in Christ, Danny Moseley. COVID took you before I could finish, but people will read your amazing story in chapter 7. I miss you, friend, but I will see you again. Your life was an inspiration. I'm grateful for your testimony and for everything I learned from you about making disciples who make disciples.

# Contents

# Contents

# Foreword

There is a word that describes the modern-day church: *intentions*. The church has good intentions. If not, she would lose identity and even her self-worth. The church has intentions to see people's lives better as they come to know God. The church has intentions of people walking in faith and victory. Yes, the church has intentions of knowing deceased members are immediately in heaven in the presence of the Lord. These are all good intentions.

But there is a word that is grossly missing in the church today: *intentionality*. We are not intentionally obeying the commands of Jesus. We are not intentionally on His mission. We are not intentionally sharing the gospel and winning lost people to saving faith in Jesus. And we are not intentionally making disciples who make disciples.

It's one thing to have good intentions but it's an entirely different thing to have intentionality. It's past time we quit feeling good about our good intentions and start getting intentional about what Jesus commanded us to do. After all, obedience is the only path to a right relationship with God. The apostle John wrote, "For this is the love of God, that we keep his commandments. And his commandments are not burdensome" (1 John 5:3).

Jesus gave a simple call, "Follow Me." But it begs the question, What does following Jesus look like? To follow Jesus means you go the way Jesus is going and you accompany Him as He goes. Following Jesus is not complicated but it is sacrificial. I see five specific things Jesus taught that describe what following Him looks like.

First, Jesus said, "If anyone would come after me, let him deny himself and take up his cross daily and follow me" (Luke 9:23). Does that verse convict you as it does me? It's not hard to understand, but it does require my all. Did you notice the first word Jesus used? "If." *If* is a conditional word. This use assumes an if-then clause. If anyone is following Jesus, he will deny self and take up his cross daily. Of course, this has a flip side; if anyone is not denying self and taking up his cross daily, He is not following Jesus.

Second, Jesus said, "If you abide in my word, you are truly my disciples, and you will know the truth, and the truth will set you free" (John 8:31–32). Did you notice the first word Jesus used again? *If* you are staying in the Word, *then* you are truly a disciple. *If* you are not staying in the Word, *then* you are not a disciple. This may strike you as rigorous, but is this not the teaching of our Lord Jesus?

Third, Jesus said, "A new commandment I give to you, that you love one another: just as I have loved you, you also are to love one another. By this all people will know that you are my disciples, if you have love for one another" (John 13:34–35). Again, we are His disciples *if* we love one another.

Fourth, Jesus said, "If you love me, you will keep my commandments" (John 14:15). Obedience is the acid test for our love of Christ. There's that word *if* again. *If* we obey Him, we love Him. *If* we do not obey Him, then we do not love

Him regardless how much we say we do. These are the hard teachings of Jesus that we must accept.

Finally, after teaching on us abiding in Him as a branch is connected to the root, Jesus said, "By this my Father is glorified, that you bear much fruit and so prove to be my disciples" (John 15:8). This last time Jesus used another two-letter word, "so." *If* we bear fruit, we show that we are His disciples. Again, this is an opposite side, *if* we do not bear fruit, *then* we show that we are not His disciples.

Is this the kind of followership that you desire? Is this the kind of biblical obedience that you long for? Is this the kind of disciple you want your church to produce?

Enter *The Greater Work*. My friend, Bill Wilks, has laid out a simple, biblical, intentional path to do what Jesus told us to do right before He ascended back to His Father—make disciples. Although well thought through, Bill doesn't write as an academic, he writes as a passionate practitioner who has been eating, breathing, and sleeping disciple-making for years. He has led his church and influenced hundreds of other congregations to make disciples who make disciples.

The word *disciple* and the word *discipline* come from the same root word. Therefore, you cannot be a disciple without some disciplines. Bill will guide you through the necessary disciplines that will develop Christ-honoring disciples and do so in the context of life-on-life, disciple-on-disciple, not starting another church program.

Too many disciple-making processes concentrate only on expanding the knowledge base of the disciple. Go to this class. Read this book. Attend this seminar. Listen to this podcast. Not Bill. His discipleship development strategy is holistic in that it develops not only the head but also the heart and hands of the believer. He wants to develop the believer so that he lives according to Mark 12:30: "You shall love the Lord your God with all your *heart* and with all your *soul* and with all your *mind* and with all your *strength*" (emphasis mine).

Here's what you need to know, the strategy Bill lays out works. It has been working in thousands of lives. Churches across America and in foreign lands are seeing life change and spiritual growth by implementing what Bill has spent years perfecting.

It's time. It's time to put intentionality behind our good intentions. The church is still the best hope the world has. And the church is at her best when she is making disciples. We must do our *Greater Work* while it is still day. We must be on a mission to fulfill our Lord's Great Commission. I highly recommend *The Greater Work*. Read it. Pass it on to your pastor, deacons, and Sunday school teachers. Let's make disciples who make disciples!

Allan Taylor
Executive Pastor of Ministries
First Baptist Concord, Knoxville, TN

# Acknowledgments

*The Greater Work* has been a long work in progress. First, I want to thank my NorthPark Family for giving me the joy to serve as your lead pastor over the past two decades and for joining me in the greater work of disciple-making. God has used you to begin a movement that is spreading across the globe. I'm thankful for the many of you who are living a lifestyle of disciple-making, and I want to thank all of you for your love, support, encouragement, and prayers.

I also want to thank our North Park staff, especially Cindy Garrett and Jane Morgan, who have proofread countless documents and corrected my many mistakes. I could not have written this book without you two wonderful ladies and the contributions you have made to *The Greater Work*.

Much appreciation goes to my three sons, Josh, Jake, and Jared, and my beautiful daughters-in-law, Kathi and Darcy, who are all living the D-Life. I have gained so much insight from each of you through our many conversations about disciple-making and from your constant encouragement. I want to express tremendous gratitude to Darcy, who helped with editing the manuscript of *The Greater Work*. I couldn't have done it without you. Thank you for the many hours of reading and the copious notes you took. Your insights were amazing. God used you to help it all come together. Also, I want to express special thanks to my son Jared with J3Collection.org for designing the awesome cover for this book. You nailed it, buddy! I love my family and appreciate you all for your commitment to *The Greater Work*.

I'm also grateful for the many pastors, churches, and missionaries who have invited us to lead D-Life Boot Camps and who have joined in the disciple-making movement. Everywhere we have been, we have made new friendships that will last a lifetime. There are too many of you to name, but I am grateful for every one of you wonderful servants of Christ. I do want to especially thank Allan Taylor, who invited us to do our very first boot camp at the First Baptist Church of Woodstock, Georgia, and who wrote the foreword for this book. I appreciate you, my friend.

Words cannot express the gratitude I have for my friend John Herring, CEO at Iron Stream Media and Life Bible Study. You took the risk to publish D-Life when it was raw and undeveloped. Your plan to develop the online format was brilliant. We had no idea that D-Life would spread the way it has, but to God be the glory. Thank you for believing in D-Life and for the investments that you, Bradley, Randy, and Marty have made to see it through. Thank you for publishing this book. I love you, my friend.

Last, but certainly not least, I am so thankful to God for my beautiful wife and best friend, Rondie Wilks. You are the greatest disciple maker I know and my true partner in ministry. We do everything together, and it has been a joy to travel the country with you doing D-Life. Thank you for believing in me and for your constant support and encouragement. I appreciate you more than words can express. I love you forever!

# Introduction

*Give a man a fish and you'll feed him for a day.*
*Teach a man to fish and you'll feed him for life.*

Coffee mugs and T-shirts. This is where you will often find the quote above. It's a well-known adage that you might also read on a church marquee or in a worship bulletin. But there is a problem—a big problem! While many Christians like the saying on a mug of joe, they don't often practice it in real life. Sadly, many Christians are content to simply give a man a fish and to feed him for a day. This presents a real dilemma for the church.

Jesus said to His would-be disciples, "Follow me, and I will make you fishers of men" (Matthew 4:19). According to Jesus, the purpose of true discipleship is to teach a man to fish.

Jesus didn't merely give out fish and chips to His disciples and feed them for a day. He taught His followers how to fish as a way of life. His purpose was not to lead a discipleship program but to cultivate disciple-making people. Jesus literally poured His life into making disciples who make disciples.

The theme of this book is disciple-making—anytime and anywhere. This is the greater work that Jesus has called His followers to do. The big idea that we will unpack in the pages of this book is that . . .

# Disciple-making is not a program; it's a lifestyle.

This one truth has the power to revitalize today's church. What if you could transform your church's discipleship program into an army of disciple-making people? What if you could transition your discipleship classes into a true disciple-making culture? This would be a game-changer for your church.

The early church was a church without walls. The one thing they knew how to do was the one thing Jesus taught them to do. He poured His short life into making disciples who would make disciples who would make disciples. This was His only strategy for how His kingdom would grow on earth. Ninety-nine percent of the ministry of the early church took place outside the walls of a building. There were no elaborate ministry programs or clever marketing schemes.

Instead, He chose twelve disciples who were very simple and common men. As they followed Him, He infected them with life, while entrusting them with a life-giving gospel. Then, He multiplied them out to go and infect others who were to go and infect others.

With no big buildings or budgets, the early church grew rapidly because it knew how to multiply. This was what Jesus had taught them to do. He didn't teach His disciples how to add but how to multiply.

Plain and simple, the early church was a grassroots disciple-making movement, and the authorities of the world could not contain it. Not even the gates of hell could prevail against it. If only the gospel had continued to spread like that, the church could have accomplished the Great Commission many centuries ago.

If the church today wants to reestablish itself as a powerful force on earth for the gospel of Christ, it must return to the movement that Jesus began. The key to global evangelism is not the megachurch, but the many churches of all sizes willing to rekindle the flames of a once powerful disciple-making movement.

I've had the joy of serving as a lead pastor for more than thirty years. For many of those years, I struggled to establish a simple and reproducible process for disciple-making. Through an in-depth study of the four Gospels, the simple disciple-making process of Jesus became clear to me.

After this study, I've developed a process called D-Life as a tool to equip and empower others for a genuine lifestyle of disciple-making. Modeled after Jesus and His six practices of discipleship, D-Life is a simple and biblical disciple-making process that cannot fail.

Recognizing its effectiveness, Life Bible Study published D-Life to make it available to others. Since that time, D-Life has spread to hundreds of churches and ministries across the United States and in several countries. Churches of all sizes have hosted D-Life training events, and my wife, Rondie, and I have traveled the country to train thousands of believers for a lifestyle of disciple-making. We have seen the light bulb come on for many who are choosing to be a part of a growing disciple-making movement.

## Defining the Greater Work

*The Greater Work* is a book about disciple-making. In the first part of this book, I will seek to define the greater work that Jesus has called us to do and examine how we have lost sight of our supreme purpose in life. We will consider the devastating consequences of this on the church and what I believe to be the missing link.

## Doing the Greater Work

In the second part of this book, we will dive deep into the solution. We will learn how to do the greater work and how to live out our supreme purpose in life. We will consider the exponential kingdom growth possible when we make disciples who make disciples. These chapters will provide believers with a very practical guide on how to live a lifestyle of disciple-making. Many books talk about disciple-making; the goal of this book is to train you how. My prayer is that reading this book will change your life. I pray that it will help you believe that you can be a disciple maker and that it will equip you for a lifestyle of disciple-making for the rest of your life.

## Devoting to the Greater Work

In the third and final part of this book, we will consider our devotion to the greater work. The time is ripe for spiritual awakening. But it will require great devotion to lead our churches away from our dependence on discipleship programs and transition to a disciple-making culture. However, this transition is crucial. An essential key to the revitalization of our churches and revival of faith in our land is a return to biblical disciple-making.

The ultimate purpose of this book is to see a global, grassroots disciple-making movement. As you read each chapter, I encourage you to bathe every page in prayer. Pray for revival in our land. Pray for the revitalization of our churches. Pray for an army of disciple-making people to return to the greater work. And pray that God, through the power of the Holy Spirit, will equip and empower you to live out your supreme purpose in life, which is to make disciples who make disciples.

If you are a pastor or ministry leader, I encourage you to use this book as a tool to train your people for a lifestyle of disciple-making. Use it for a small group study or a larger training event. Discussion questions are provided at the end of each chapter.

You may also want to purchase D-Life Online or the *D-Life Journal* for your study groups. With these tools, you place the power to live a lifestyle of disciple-making at everyone's fingertips. The content includes four full years of Bible reading plans, Scripture memory verses, and weekly study guides for your discipleship groups, or D-Groups. These tools serve as a valuable resource to those who desire to lead a D-Group (to view samples of these materials, see appendixes 1 and 2).

In addition, Rondie and I have led D-Life Boot Camps for many churches, ministries, and associations across the country. A boot camp will provide four hours of intense training for living a lifestyle of disciple-making. We would love to come and lead D-Life training for your ministry.

For more information or to purchase D-Life Online or the *D-Life Journal*, go to www.livethedlife.com.

To schedule a D-Life training event for your ministry, please contact us at:

Bill Wilks | bill@livethedlife.com
Rondie Wilks | rondie@livethedlife.com

# 🔍 Discussion Questions for a Small Group Study

1. As you read this book, what do you hope to take away from this study? What well-known adage is quoted at the beginning of this book, and what observations did the author make concerning the church? Why do you agree or disagree with these observations?

2. What is the "big idea" of this book? What do you think would happen if you could transform your church's discipleship program into an army of disciple-making people? What would happen if you could transition your discipleship classes into a true disciple-making culture? How could this be a game-changer for your church?

3. In what ways was the early church a church without walls? How does this compare to the church today? What one main thing did Jesus teach His disciples to do? According to the author, what was the reason for the rapid growth of the early church? Why do you agree or disagree with this assessment?

4. What did the author say that today's church must do to reestablish itself as a powerful force on earth for the gospel of Christ? How can a church rekindle the flames of the great disciple-making movement that was experienced by the early church? In what ways can you contribute to this?

5. In praying for a global, grassroots, disciple-making movement, what is implied by the word grassroots? What is implied about the word movement? What specific things did the author ask for you to pray

about as you go through this study? Will you commit to pray for these things?

**Closing Prayer:** O God, hear our prayer. We pray for revival in our land, for the revitalization of your churches, and for an army of disciple-making people to rise and return to the greater work.

# PART 1

# DEFINING THE GREATER WORK

# CHAPTER 1

# The Greater Work

*And he said to them, "Follow me, and I*
*will make you fishers of men."*
—Matthew 4:19

*And Jesus came and said to them, "All authority in heaven and on earth*
*has been given to me. Go therefore and make disciples of all nations,*
*baptizing them in the name of the Father and of the Son and of the*
*Holy Spirit, teaching them to observe all that I have commanded you.*
*And behold, I am with you always, to the end of the age."*
—Matthew 28:18–20

*Truly, truly, I say to you, whoever believes in me will also do the works*
*that I do; and greater works than these will he do, because I am going to*
*the Father.*
—John 14:12

Everyone lives for something. What do you live for? What gives your life meaning? What is your purpose?

Many people struggle to know what their purpose is. Like a sailboat without a sail, they drift through life without a clear sense of direction. They may find their identity in their profession or position in life, but struggle to find any real meaning in it all.

In light of life's brevity, it's extremely important to find clarity in this. Life is a vapor—here today and gone tomorrow. The longer you travel aimlessly through life, the greater the danger that you will completely miss your purpose. At the very least, your life will not live up to its potential.

Some think they know what their purpose is, but they are aiming for the wrong target. Even if they hit the bull's-eye, their true purpose in life remains unfulfilled. Perhaps this is where a great many in the church are today. They may not know what is missing, but something clearly is. Their lives might appear on target, but they are totally missing the mark of what God has in mind for them. The goal of the Christian life is not simply to have a purpose but to live out God's purpose. What good is it to be an excellent marksman if you are aiming in the wrong direction? The important question to answer is not, "Does my life have a purpose?" Of course, it does. But the important question is, "What is God's purpose for my life?"

Where can we find the answer to this? If you do a Google search on "purpose in life," you will get close to a billion hits in less than a second. You will read endless opinions ranging from finding your true self to loving others as yourself. Though many articles express strong sentiments on the subject, the sheer volume of ideas is likely to leave you with more confusion than clarity.

Is there a reliable resource with a decisive word on the matter? Is there someone who can tell you plainly what your purpose is? Thankfully, there is!

Jesus Christ is our living Lord. Every word He speaks is absolute truth and has complete authority. He is the only one who can tell you what your purpose is, and He speaks clearly on the matter.

## The Big Truth

The big truth is that your purpose is one main thing. According to Jesus, it's two words—"make disciples." Every believer in Christ lives under the crystal-clear mandate of His Great Commission. There are no exceptions. No matter your age, gender, or nationality, Jesus has called you to a lifestyle of disciple-making.

Your profession is not your purpose. It may be a secondary purpose that God has for you, and it certainly is a blessing from God as a source of provision for you and your family. However, it doesn't matter if you are a butcher, a baker, or a candlestick maker, your profession is not your ultimate objective. According to Jesus, your supreme purpose is to make disciples.

We see this plainly in both the first and final commands of Jesus to His followers. We also see it in the powerful example of His own life. Disciple-making is the greater work that He has called all of us to do.

## To Make Disciples Is Jesus' First Command to His Followers

In Mathew 4:19, we find Jesus' first command to His followers. He said to them, "Follow me, and I will make you fishers of men." This verse is the Great Commission before the Great Commission. With a beautiful brevity of words, Jesus makes three clear and powerful declarations about our purpose in life.

First, He said, "Follow me." This is life's greatest invitation. These two powerful words present you with a clear call to salvation. In the Greek, this is an adverb of place that literally means to "come here" or "come after me." Forgiveness of sins, reconciliation with God, and eternal life in heaven are just a few of the bountiful blessings of God's amazing grace when you heed the call to follow after Jesus in faith.

Second, Jesus stated that He will make you into something new. The Greek word translated "make" means to form or produce. It means to bring about something new or different. Here, Jesus makes it clear that to come after Him is life-changing. It's transformational. He will form you into something that you are not yet. Then, He clearly marked the target.

Third, Jesus gave the end product of this transformational process, which is to become "fishers of men." This was Jesus' way of communicating to a group of common fishermen that His followers become fishers of men—that His disciples become disciple-makers. Jesus made it clear. When you heed the call to follow Him, His purpose for you is to be a disciple who makes disciples.

This leads to an important point. If you're not fishing for men, then you are not following Jesus. Jesus makes disciples who make disciples. He doesn't make any other kind, and He doesn't call you to make any other kind. A major principle we learn from Jesus is that disciple-making is a multiplying process.

## To Make Disciples Is Jesus' Final Command to His Followers

Jesus' final command to His followers is found in Matthew 28:18–20. It's a well-known passage that we like to call the "Great

Suggestion." Well, not really. We call it the Great Commission, but most believers seem to think of it as a suggestion. However, the Great Commission is not a suggestion!

For three years, Jesus carefully invested His life into His followers. He diligently equipped and empowered them to be disciples who make disciples. Then, He took up a cross and willingly gave His life for them. Three days later, He came out of His tomb and was resurrected to new life. For the next forty days, Jesus met with His disciples and gave them final instructions. Before His ascension back to the Father, Jesus stood on a mountain in His resurrected body and said, "All authority in heaven and on earth has been given to me. Go therefore and make disciples of all nations, baptizing them in the name of the Father and of the Son and of the Holy Spirit, teaching them to observe all that I have commanded you. And behold, I am with you always, to the end of the age" (Matthew 28:18-20).

Backed by all the authority in heaven and on earth, our Risen Lord commanded His followers to do one thing—"make disciples." He could have said anything here, but His purpose for us was plainly stated. There is only one verb in the Great Commission. The literal rendering of the Greek language is: "Going therefore, disciple all the nations." The word "make" is implied from the text and the word "disciple" is an imperative verb of command. These are Jesus' final words on earth and His instructions are clear.

After giving His followers an explicit mandate, Jesus informed them on how to accomplish it. In the Great Commission, these three descriptive participles tell us how to make disciples. He said that we are to make disciples by going, by baptizing, and by teaching.

To begin, we are to make disciples by going to them. Jesus did not instruct us to build buildings and to make disciples of those who come inside the walls. Instead, He taught us to go meet people on their turf and to make disciples wherever they are. Disciple-making was never meant to be a program of the church that takes place inside a classroom. It was meant to be the lifestyle of every believer that can take place anytime and anywhere. As we go and everywhere we go, we are to make disciples.

Next, we are to make disciples by baptizing them. Engaging in frequent gospel conversations with those outside the church is a vital part of disciple-making. As we carefully and intentionally lead others to Christ, we must encourage them to profess their faith in Him through water baptism. For new believers to unite with a local church through water baptism is an essential step in the discipleship process.

Finally, we are to make disciples by teaching them to observe all Christ has commanded us to do. Teaching is a labor of love that involves both verbal instruction and visual examples. It is so much more than merely transferring knowledge. It also involves a diligent mentoring process as modeled by Jesus and later by the apostle Paul. Paul referred to the Galatian believers as "my little children, for whom I am again in the anguish [or labor] of childbirth until Christ is formed in you!" (Galatians 4:19). To see a new believer transformed into the image of Christ is the ultimate goal of discipleship and one that will require your full attention and devotion. Clearly, this involves an intentional process for teaching them to make other disciples. Disciples who make other disciples are not made by accident. It must be intentional.

Once again, we see in the Great Commission that discipleship is a multiplying process. Like two great bookends to the earthly ministry of Jesus, both His first and final commands stress the multiplying mandate of true discipleship. Our goal is not merely to make converts for Christ, but to make disciples who make disciples. Apart from multiplication, there is no real discipleship.

## To Make Disciples Is Jesus' Great Example for His Followers

Are you convinced? No matter who you are or what your profession, your supreme purpose in life is to make disciples. Yes, your chief end is to glorify God, but how can you glorify Him if you ignore His Great Commission?

If you are not convinced, then consider this—Jesus not only commanded us to make disciples, but He modeled it for us. He gave us an example to follow.

As a young man at the age of thirty, Jesus began His earthly ministry with a forty-day fast. He spent time in the wilderness fasting, praying, and contending with the devil. With only three short years of ministry before He would die on a cross, He wanted to use His time wisely and do His Father's will. Consequently, He accomplished more in three years than any other will achieve in a lifetime.

After completing His fast, Jesus' first priority was to call a small group of men to be His disciples. He went to each man individually and called each one "so that they might be with him and he might send them out to preach" (Mark 3:14). Twelve men accepted the invitation to become His disciples.

They left everything to follow after Him and to be a part of His discipleship group—His D-Group.

The remarkable thing about these men is that they were common men. They were not prophets or priests. They were not wealthy or powerful. As far as we know, they were not even well educated. They were simple, blue-collar workers consisting of a government worker who collected taxes for Rome, a political revolutionary who hated tax collectors, and a pair of brothers who were hard-working fishermen, to name a few. They were not the sharpest knives in the drawer; rather, they consistently struggled with issues of envy, pride, jealousy, doubt, insecurity, and recklessness. Yet from this ragtag group of social misfits, Jesus launched a grassroots disciple-making movement called the church.

It seems obvious that Jesus called these men to be His first disciples to show us that anyone can be a disciple-maker. If they could do it, you can do it. Anyone who follows after Jesus can live out his or her supreme purpose in life regardless of one's gifts or abilities.

Think about it. Jesus did many good things in His three years of ministry. He healed the sick, performed many miracles, cared for the poor, taught the masses, and confronted religious hypocrisy. Yet one thing was His priority, one thing demanded His full attention. He literally poured His life into turning ordinary fishermen into fishers of men and transforming twelve misfits into disciple-makers. Second only to His sacrificial death on the cross, making disciples was Jesus' supreme purpose in life. It was His greater work!

## To Make Disciples Is Jesus' Greater Work for His Followers

Just before His crucifixion, Jesus met with His disciples in an upper room. He said many important things to them, but one thing He said was truly amazing. According to John 14:12, Jesus said, "Truly, truly, I say to you, whoever believes in me will also do the works that I do; and greater works than these will he do, because I am going to the Father." What did He mean by this? How can anyone ever do "greater works" than the Son of God?

These words of Jesus have often been misunderstood and misinterpreted. Some suggest that we will do greater miracles than Jesus. Really? Jesus walked on water, spoke violent storms out of existence, fed great multitudes with a child's lunch, turned water into exquisite wine, healed all manner of diseases, and even raised the dead on multiple occasions. I've never seen anyone do greater miracles than Jesus, and I'm certain I never will.

But this is not what Jesus said. He didn't say that we would do greater miracles than Him, but greater works. The Greek word used here is *ergon*. It speaks of the works, deeds, or tasks that one normally does. Second only to His sacrificial death on the cross, what was the one main work that Jesus did during His three years of ministry? It was the work of making disciples. He poured His life into His discipleship group of twelve men.

Disciple-making is the greater work. What else could it be? Apart from His death on the cross, it was the one main work that Jesus did in His time on earth. It laid the foundation for His death on the cross. Jesus is "the Lamb of God, who takes away the sin of the world" (John 1:29), but how will the world know about this Lamb and His sacrifice without an unbroken chain of disciples who make disciples?

Before He went back to the Father, He promised to send a Helper—the Holy Spirit. It makes sense, doesn't it? The Holy Spirit is the Spirit of the greatest disciple-maker who ever lived, and He dwells in us. He is our Divine Helper. Jesus sent Him to us so that we could do an even greater work of disciple-making than He did. Jesus was only one person, but we are many. Through the Holy Spirit, the DNA of a disciple-maker is in our blood and it flows through our veins. Because of the power of the Holy Spirit, we can do an even greater work than Jesus of making disciples who make disciples. Until He returns, this is our final command. It's our greater work.

## Final Thoughts

You may be thinking, but what about His other works? What about His divine miracles? Doesn't He still do works of miracles? What about social justice? Didn't Jesus come to proclaim good news to the poor, liberty to the captives, sight to the blind, and freedom to the oppressed? Shouldn't these things be included in His greater works?

Absolutely! Here is where we see a most beautiful and powerful truth about genuine discipleship. In authentic disciple-making, all these great works are joined together into one process. The message of the kingdom, the ministry of the kingdom, and the miracles of the kingdom are woven together into a beautiful vestment of His marvelous grace. They cannot and must not be separated!

Look closely at Jesus' example. He called His disciples to be fishers of men and they left everything to follow Him. Immediately afterward, the Bible says:

And he went throughout all Galilee, teaching in their synagogues and proclaiming the gospel of the kingdom and healing every disease and every affliction among the people. So his fame spread throughout all Syria, and they brought him all the sick, those afflicted with various diseases and pains, those oppressed by demons, those having seizures, and paralytics, and he healed them. And great crowds followed him from Galilee and the Decapolis, and from Jerusalem and Judea, and from beyond the Jordan. (Matthew 4:23–25)

Do you see it? Look closely at these words. He went out with His disciples "proclaiming the gospel of the kingdom" and "healing every disease and affliction." They brought Him all "the sick" and "those afflicted" and "those oppressed" and "He healed them." So His fame spread and great crowds followed Him. This is true discipleship.

As Jesus led His disciples outside the walls of the synagogue to proclaim the message of the kingdom, they watched Him touch the leper, heal the blind and lame, feed the hungry, and show compassion for the sinner. They learned from Him that the message, the ministry, and the miracles of His kingdom are a package deal. You can't have one without the other.

We see in Jesus' example a clear picture of authentic disciple-making; we see a perfect model of the greater work! As a result, Jesus launched a disciple-making movement called the church. It was an unstoppable movement of common people who were big on social justice and sharing the good news. With no big buildings or budgets, His disciples multiplied greatly, and the fame of Jesus spread across the earth.

For the first three and a half centuries of church history, this movement could not be stopped. The entire world was within reach of the gospel, but tragically, it did stop. A grassroots movement was replaced by professional clergy. Disciple-making people were replaced with ecclesiastical programs. Consequently, the movement died. A church that once made Jesus famous was replaced by one that has often made Him infamous, and dark ages followed.

Throughout history, there have been times when godly people have tried to revive the movement, but it has never returned to the great force it once was when it turned the world upside down for Christ. We see the effect on the church today. The reason why many Christ-followers are weak on social justice is that they haven't been properly discipled. Weak discipleship is the reason why many never share the gospel of Christ or see His great miracles. The tragic result is that the fame of Jesus fails to spread and great crowds do not follow. Everything rises and falls on Christlike discipleship.

Herein lies the great dilemma for the church today. Over two thousand years ago Jesus said, "Go and make disciples of all nations," yet today there remain over five thousand unreached people groups with billions of people in our world who have never even heard about Jesus. In America, the vast majority of our churches are declining or dying. An unstoppable disciple-making movement has been replaced with ineffective discipleship programs and most believers never live out their supreme purpose in life. For most, the Great Commission is merely a great suggestion.

How did this happen? What has become of the greater work that Jesus said we would do? Why have so many churches lost sight of their great mission? Why do most believers fail to live out their purpose in life? Is there a solution to this great dilemma?

I believe there is. However, there is a broken net that must be mended. In the next chapter, we will learn about "The Broken Net."

# 🔍 Discussion Questions for a Small Group Study

1. Why is it important to know your purpose in life? How can you find your purpose? According to the author, what two words spoken by Jesus define your purpose in life, and what two passages in the Bible were given to support this? Why do you agree or disagree?

2. Why do many believers treat the Great Commission as a good suggestion? What is the one verb in the Great Commission and what does this verb command us to do? What three words in the Great Commission instruct us how to make disciples and how can we apply these instructions in personal disciple-making?

3. In what ways did Jesus model the Great Commission in His own life? Read John 14:12. What truly amazing claim did Jesus make in this verse? According to the author, what is the greater work that Jesus was referring to? Why do you agree or disagree?

4. In the example of Jesus, how are the message, the ministry, and the miracles of the kingdom all woven together in disciple-making? Why is weak disciple-making a reason why many believers are weak on social justice and in sharing the gospel? In the church, why does everything rise or fall on Christlike disciple-making?

5. Right now, could you honestly say that you are living out your supreme purpose in life? Do you treat that Great Commission like it's a good suggestion? Why or why not? How do you hope this book will help you with this?

**Closing Prayer:** Heavenly Father, thank You for calling us to be disciples of Jesus Christ. Help us to understand and embrace our supreme purpose in life, which is to make disciples who make disciples.

# CHAPTER 2

# The Broken Net

*And Simon answered, "Master, we toiled all night and took nothing!
But at your word I will let down the nets." And when they had done
this, they enclosed a large number of fish, and their nets were breaking.*
—Luke 5:5–6

I once heard about a man who was a successful corporate
headhunter. His job was to find gifted, young executives for
leading businesses. When he would interview candidates, he
would try to make them feel comfortable. He would engage
them in small talk, get them to kick back, loosen their ties, and
relax. Then, out of the blue, he would hit them with a question
that always caught them off guard. "So tell me," he would ask,
"What is your purpose in life?" Most were more than ready to
share their impressive resumes, but no one had prepared them
for this subject. He relished in watching them squirm in their
seats as they struggled to find answers to this all-important
question.

On one occasion, the man brought in a young professional
for an interview and casually led him to feel relaxed. At just
the right moment, he dropped the question, "So tell me, what
is your purpose in life?" Without hesitation, the young man

replied, "My purpose in life is to go to heaven and to take as many people with me as I can." For the first time in his career, the corporate headhunter was caught off guard. He was totally unprepared for the man's answer.

I can't remember when I first heard this story, but I've never forgotten it. Here was a young man who understood that his purpose in life was not his profession. He knew that his greater work was to make disciples. We need more like him in the church today.

The problem is that disciple-making is not a strength for most believers or most churches. This should greatly concern us. The vast majority of churches in America are either stagnant or declining. Of the few that are growing, a good portion is from Christians leaving other churches or from "church hopping." Though it's exciting to see new people and families come into the church, I long to see new conversions to Christ rather than transfer growth. New conversion growth is Great Commission growth. It's the only kind of growth that advances the kingdom of God on earth and promotes revival in our land.

I truly believe the key to revival is not found in the megachurch model but in the many churches of all sizes that reside in every major city and rural community in our land. When these churches revitalize and recapture the disciple-making movement that Jesus began, we can turn the world upside down for the gospel of Christ once again. To see this, we must mend the broken net.

One of the first interactions between Jesus and Peter is recounted in the Gospel of Luke. A large crowd was pressing in on Jesus to hear Him teach the Word of God. Jesus climbed aboard Simon Peter's fishing boat and asked him to push out a little from the land. Jesus sat down and taught the people from the boat. When Jesus had finished teaching, He said to Simon Peter, "Put out into the deep and let down your nets for a catch" (Luke 5:4). A tired and weary Peter took exception with Jesus telling him how to fish. He said, "Master, we toiled all night and took nothing" (Luke 5:5). In other words, I think Peter was saying, "Master, you should stick to preaching and let us handle the fishing!" Nevertheless, he did exactly as Jesus had said and he let down the nets. According to Luke, when they had done this, they caught such a large number of fish that "their nets were breaking" (Luke 5:6). There were so many fish that they had to recruit their partners in another boat to help them haul them in. When they had filled up both boats, the haul of fish was so large that the boats began to sink.

When Simon Peter saw this, it wrecked him. He fell down before Jesus and said, "Depart from me, for I am a sinful man, O Lord" (Luke 5:8). I believe this was when Peter realized who Jesus really was and surrendered to Him as Lord. I think this was the moment he experienced genuine salvation. At this point, Jesus reminded him of his purpose and of the greater work that He was calling him to do. He said to Simon Peter, "Do not be afraid; from now on you will be catching men" (Luke 5:10). After the disciples brought their boats to land, they left everything to follow Jesus.

## The Great Catch

The great catch of fish that the disciples hauled in was because of their obedience to Jesus. They had been fishing all night using their own methods and caught nothing. Though they were reluctant at first, they did exactly as Jesus said and they were astonished at their great catch of fish. If they had not obeyed, there would have been no fish. They would have toiled to no avail. Peter and the rest of the disciples learned a great lesson that day. It is a sin to think that you know more than Jesus and that your ways of doing things are better than His. They learned that His way is the right way. No matter how impractical it may seem, His way is always best.

I believe their great catch of fish was a picture of the disciple-making movement that Jesus would soon begin through them. He would transform these fishermen into fishers of men. He would equip and empower them to be disciples who make disciples. He would train them for the greater work. Through their obedience to be disciple-makers, Jesus would build His church and the gates of hell would not prevail against it.

How awesome would it be to see a great catch of people for the gospel of Christ like the one we see in this story? What if churches today began to overflow, not with transfer growth, but with Kingdom growth? What if the lost began coming to Christ to such a degree that our churches could not contain them? Do we even think this is possible today? Are we like Peter who was reluctant to believe this could happen?

## The Breaking Nets

I find it interesting that Luke, under the inspiration of the Holy Spirit, added one small, seemingly insignificant detail to this story. As the disciples attempted to haul in this large catch of fish, Luke says, "Their nets were breaking" (Luke 5:6). I don't believe this is insignificant.

The breaking nets reveal that the disciples were not fully prepared for the greater work that Jesus was calling them to do. They were not ready to become disciples who make disciples. To be so would require them to leave everything and follow

Jesus. They would have to learn to trust and obey Him even when it seemed impractical. The breaking nets would have to be mended.

For the next three years, Jesus literally poured His life into these twelve men to equip them for this work. He said to Peter, "Do not be afraid; from now on you will be catching men" (Luke 5:10). Jesus' plan for His disciples was to mend the broken nets.

## The Common Misconceptions About Discipleship

For the church today, the broken net represents some very common misconceptions that people have about discipleship. As long as we think that we know more than Jesus and that our ways of doing things are better than His, we are unlikely to see this great catch of people for the gospel of Christ. Like Peter, we must exchange our misconceptions about discipleship for doing exactly as Jesus has said.

First, many think of discipleship as mere evangelism. For them, it's all about sharing the gospel with the lost and seeking to lead others to Christ. Over the years, great evangelism tools like *The Four Spiritual Laws*, *The Roman Road*, *FAITH Evangelism*, and *Evangelism Explosion*, have been used to train people for evangelism. I had the privilege to serve as Lead Pastor for four years at Greenbriar Road Baptist Church in Anniston, Alabama. During my time there, we were a "clinic church" for *Evangelism Explosion*. Not only were many of our members well trained in evangelism, but we also hosted people from around the country who came to be trained by our people. Some of the most sincere and dedicated "soul winners" I've ever met were in that church. Needless to say, over my four years there, we saw many people profess faith in Christ through our evangelism efforts. I had the joy of baptizing many of them. However, we saw many converts but few disciples. Our baptism numbers looked great, but I can't honestly say that we were making disciples who make disciples. Don't take this wrong. I love to share my faith and I rejoice over every single convert to Christ. Personal evangelism is a vital part of disciple-making. However, evangelism alone is not discipleship. Great numbers of people have been led to pray "the sinner's prayer," but have never matured in their faith, become ambassadors of social justice, or reproduced other disciples. This is a major concern and a great tear in the disciple-making net.

Second, many think that discipleship is all about going deep into Bible study. For them, it's all about listening to anointed teachers, reading volumes of Christian books, and participating in small group Bible studies. Great teachers like John Piper, David Platt, Henry Blackaby, Beth Moore, Kay Arthur, and Priscilla Shirer are household names. Indeed, God has given the church many gifted teachers for building up the body of Christ, and we would all agree that going deep into Bible study is extremely important. The issue is that we complete great studies by anointed teachers, and we think that discipleship consists merely of participating in the next study. We will say, "That was an awesome study. I can't wait to sign up for the next one." As a result, many in our churches are more biblically literate than most third-world missionaries. However, they don't know what to do with all their knowledge. They just keep taking it in without giving it out. This is a problem. Attending Bible studies alone is not discipleship.

Let's be clear. Discipleship does involve both evangelism and teaching, but we must not separate the two. The discipling process of Jesus joined together both evangelism and teaching in a relational small group environment that also included mentoring, accountability, and, most importantly, multiplication. In contrast, a great majority of spiritually educated believers today fail to reproduce as disciple-makers. This, too, is a major concern and a great tear in the disciple-making net.

Third, many think of discipleship as a program of the church. If you were to ask the average church member if their church had a discipleship program, most, if not all, would say that they do. Some would go on to tell you how great their discipleship program is and what great Bible studies they offer. They might even invite you to attend. However, if you were to ask them what role they serve in their church, you would get answers like usher, greeter, teacher, deacon, choir member, band member, ministry leader, committee member, and golf cart driver, to name a few. "What's wrong with that," you ask, "Isn't service a part of discipleship?" Absolutely, service is an essential part of discipleship, but here is the problem. When you ask believers about their role of service in the church, you never hear anyone say, "I'm a disciple-maker." Disciple-making is our supreme purpose in life. It's our greater work. Yet, no one seems to see disciple-making as his or her primary role. Instead, churches with well-planned "discipleship" programs tend to view everything they do as discipleship. If everything we do is discipleship, then nothing really is. Jesus did not invite twelve men to join a discipleship program. He trained them to be disciple-making people.

Do you see the difference? With twelve simple men, Jesus launched a disciple-making movement that exploded upon the world. In comparison, the church today has discipleship programs, but few disciple-making people. Who came up with this idea? What led us to believe that we could improve on Jesus' plan of discipleship? As long as we think that we know more than Jesus and that our ways of doing things are better than His, we will toil in vain. We must exchange our misconceptions about discipleship for doing exactly as Jesus has said.

## The Need for a Process of Multiplication for Discipleship

As we have already seen, Jesus made it clear that discipleship is a multiplying process. Jesus made disciples who made disciples; He didn't make any other kind. Apart from multiplication, there is no real discipleship. Multiplication is the key to reaching our world for Christ. However, most churches today lack a simple process for equipping believers to make and to multiply disciples. This is a gaping hole in the disciple-making net!

My wife, Rondie, is my partner in disciple-making. She is not only an amazing pastor's wife but is a passionate disciple-maker herself. Together, we have traveled the country to train people in many churches and associations for a lifestyle of disciple-making. A few years ago, we set up our D-Life exhibit at the Jacksonville Pastor's Conference at the First Baptist Church in Jacksonville, Florida. We had the opportunity to discuss discipleship with many wonderful pastors. There was one question that we tried to ask each one: "Do you have any ministry in your church that is truly multiplying?" Of about a hundred pastors that we spoke with, not a single one said they had any ministry in their church that was truly multiplying. Though this answer is tragic, it was not entirely unexpected.

Herein lies the problem. Few believers today live a lifestyle of making and multiplying disciples because the church fails to equip them for it. For the most part, we are attempting to reach the world by addition and we simply cannot keep pace. Jesus' plan for reaching the world was not one of addition. If it had been, He could have done it better than anyone. In His three years of ministry, He could have preached the Sermon on the Mount every week and offered spirited evangelistic invitations. I'm sure that thousands would have responded to His anointed preaching, but this was not His plan.

Instead, He envisioned the exponential growth of His kingdom through the remarkable process of multiplication. As a result, He invested His life into twelve very ordinary men. There was no brave heart to be found in this bunch. But Jesus said, "Follow me." He promised that He would make them into something new. And that is exactly what He did. The disciple-making flame that Jesus ignited in these men still burns today, but ever so faintly. Yet, the wind of the Spirit is blowing. Do you feel it? It's time to repair the net! It's time to rekindle the flame!

Dream with me. What if we began to embrace disciple-making as our supreme purpose in life instead of a program of the church? What if we truly began to make disciples who make disciples? What if we began to rekindle the flame of a grassroots disciple-making movement? This would change everything!

In some places, this movement has already begun. In certain areas of China, India, and Africa the movement is thriving. In Africa alone, Christianity has grown from 9 to nearly 48 percent in the last one hundred years.[1]

I recently had lunch with a missionary friend. With great excitement, he shared with me how the impoverished church in Africa was experiencing a great revival through the simple process of multiplying disciples. He said that he longs to see the revitalization of this movement in America, and many others have the same desire. Every week, Rondie and I talk with pastors from across our country who want to be a part of a new disciple-making movement.

The Holy Spirit is igniting in the hearts of many a burning passion for the greater work. However, there are broken nets that must be mended and there is one big question that must be answered. We will consider this big question in our next chapter.

## 🔍 Discussion Questions for a Small Group Study

1. Why do you think that disciple-making is not a strength for most Christians? Would you consider it to be one of your strengths? Why or why not? For what reasons do you think the majority of churches in America today are either stagnant or declining?

2. What three misconceptions about discipleship did the author give? Why does genuine discipleship involve more than just evangelism? Why does genuine discipleship require more than just teaching the Bible? What is the difference between having a discipleship program and having disciple-making people?

3. According to the author, if everything we do in the church is called discipleship, then nothing really is. Why do you agree or disagree? What does it mean for a church to have a disciple-making culture? How is this different from having a discipleship program? Which one do you think that your church has and why?

4.  Why is the multiplication of disciples the key to reaching our world for Christ? The author says, "Apart from multiplication there is no real discipleship." Why do you agree or disagree with this statement? In what ways did Jesus model a multiplying process of disciple-making?
5.  What would a disciple-making movement look like in your church? How would such a movement impact your community? In what ways would you be willing to contribute to this movement?

**Closing Prayer:** Heavenly Father, thank you for sending your Son to save us from our sin. But people cannot know about our great Savior unless we tell them. Please rekindle the flame of the disciple-making movement of the early church and let it begin in us.

# CHAPTER 3

# The Big Question

*When Jesus saw him lying there and knew that he had already been there a long time, he said to him, "Do you want to be healed?"*
—John 5:6

The first time I met him, he said, "Hi, I'm Wirt, like dirt." I never forgot his name after that. How could you forget Wirt, like dirt? Wirt is a simple man—hard-working, self-taught, and a bit rough around the edges. Though he's now a very successful businessman, he didn't grow up that way. He had to work for it. He got his start selling used tires in the inner city of Birmingham, Alabama. He discovered a great market and eventually opened several refurbished tire stores in some pretty rough areas of the city. Realizing this might not be the best environment for a family business, he taught himself a new occupation. Wirt, like dirt, learned horticulture. Stepping out in faith, he switched from selling old used tires to beautiful new plants. Warren Family Garden Center is now one of the largest plant, shrub, and tree nurseries in the Birmingham area.

Wirt Warren became my friend. I invited him to join my D-Group and met with him weekly for Bible study and spiritual accountability. He was a relatively new Christian who had not grown up in the church. Our small group of men loved Wirt's unpretentious faith and unbridled hunger for God's Word. After walking through the New Testament with Wirt for an entire year, I explained to him the multiplying process of discipleship. I encouraged him to step out and lead his own D-Group. Wirt is a man's man, and I knew that God could use him to lead other men in discipleship. Teary-eyed, he thanked me for teaching him how to make disciples.

Wirt, like dirt, is now a disciple-maker. He reaches men in his D-Group that others might not be able to reach. He also leads a D-Group of teenage boys every week before school at a local restaurant. He calls me frequently to discuss issues that arise in his group and to share exciting stories about discipleship.

The beautiful thing about discipleship is anyone can be trained to be a disciple-maker. It doesn't require a seminary degree. It's not just for those with the gift of teaching or the gift of evangelism. Jesus kept it simple so it could be for everyone. If the common men He called to be His disciples could learn to do it, then anyone can.

I have great respect for my friend Wirt. He is not only a successful businessman and loving family man, but first and foremost, he's a disciple-maker. He gets it. His profession is not his purpose in life, disciple-making is.

Here is the big question. Are you willing to become a disciple-maker if someone could train you how? Today's church harbors many who are comfortable in their positions and unwilling to be transformed into something new.

During a feast of the Jews, Jesus went up to Jerusalem. As usual, He didn't spend His time rubbing shoulders with the rich and famous. He wasn't there looking for a photo op with a prestigious Pharisee or a rich lawyer who might give a financial blessing to His ministry. He made a straight line to those in need. He visited a pool below the temple with five roofed colonnades called the Pool of Bethesda. There he found the dregs of society—the blind, the lame, and the paralyzed. All around the pool lay a multitude of helpless invalids, the kind more proper people would rather avoid. But not Jesus, He went straight to them. He found a man who had been an invalid for thirty-eight years. When Jesus saw him, He knew instantly that he had been in that state for a long time. Then He asked the man what seems like a pointless question. Jesus said to him, "Do you want to be healed" (John 5:6)? Of course he did, right? After thirty-eight years of misery, you would think the man would have cried out, "Yes, Lord, please heal me!" But instead, he began to make excuses about having no one to put him in the pool and about some mysterious stirring of the water.

We see in this that Jesus' question was not pointless at all. In fact, it was an important one for the man to answer. Misery loves company and the man had a lot of company. He had become accustomed to living from the charity of others. He made many friends at those colonnades and he had found comfort living by the water. This was all he knew. Perhaps he was too comfortable with where he was to be transformed into something new. The big question for him to answer was: "Do you want to be healed?" This is a big question for today's church as well.

## The Sad Condition of the Church

The church in America is not well. Like the man by the Pool of Bethesda, we offer excuses for our sad condition, but we desperately need revival. In my own denomination, the

Southern Baptist Convention, that for many years was our nation's largest Protestant denomination, the following has been observed:

- Baptisms continue to decline. Overall, baptisms have reached a historic low—around how many people were baptized by the denomination back in the 1940s.[2]
- Southern Baptist membership is at its lowest in thirty years.[3]
- High-profile articles on sexual abuse in the Southern Baptist churches have exposed numerous leaders in those churches and agencies who had been convicted of or taken plea deals in sex crimes involving hundreds of victims.[4]

These disturbing trends should grieve our hearts. Declining baptisms and widespread sexual abuse are very painful realities. Though they are unpleasant to consider, it is imperative we deal with them.

The news for the American church, in general, doesn't get any better. The fastest-growing religious group in America today is the nones. Who are the nones? They are not devout Catholic women, but they are the rapidly rising group of people in the US whose religious affiliation is "none." When they are asked about their religious preference, their answer is not Baptist, Methodist, Pentecostal, Catholic, or even nondenominational. It's simply "none." According to James Emery White, the nones outnumber Southern Baptists and are eclipsed only by Catholics as the nation's second-largest religious group.[5] In his book, *The Rise of the Nones*, White says:

To put this in perspective, consider that the number of *nones* in the 1930s and '40s hovered around 5 percent. By 1990 that number had only risen to 8 percent, a mere 3 percent rise in over half a century. Between 1990 and 2008—just eighteen years—the number of *nones* leaped from 8.1 percent to 15 percent. Then, in just four short years, it climbed to 20 percent, representing one of every five Americans.[6]

White believes that the United States is swiftly moving along the same path as the UK, where the nones comprise 25 percent of the population.[7] With the recent finding by the National Study of Youth and Religion that a full one-third of US adults under the age of thirty do not identify with any religion,[8] the spiritual decline and darkness that has overtaken Europe are quickly moving our way.

In another heart-probing book, *The Great Evangelical Recession*, John Dickerson stresses the point that there are not nearly as many evangelical Christians in America as we were once led to believe. Dickerson says, "At best, according to the most optimistic reports, we are two in every ten Americans."[9] Citing multiple sources, he makes a strong case that evangelical believers comprise only between 7 to 9 percent of the US population.[10] In agreement with James White, Dickerson states:

As the U.S. church shrinks, the number of nonreligious and secular Americans is skyrocketing. If you took a group of one hundred evangelicals today, there would be a corresponding group of two hundred overtly secular nonbelievers. The two hundred overt secularists include stated atheists, agnostics, and non-religious. More significant than the outnumbering is the breakdown by age. The percentage of evangelicals decreases with each younger generation, while the percentage of agnostics and atheists increases in younger generations. The net effect over time will be a tsunami-like culture shift, as the older generations pass away.[11]

This information may catch you by surprise if you've read recent headlines about America's booming megachurches. When we read or hear testimonies about these churches, it's easy to assume that all is well, and faith is on the rise. However, Dickerson cites a study by the Hartford Institute for Religion and Research, indicating that at least three in four of those comprising the "booming growth" of the megachurch left another church. This means that the majority of growth in these churches is not the result of new conversions to Christ but the transfer of existing Christians. Seventy-five percent are coming from other churches, with the result that total attendance at all evangelical churches is declining in almost every state.[12] White adds that if this trend doesn't change, "small churches will keep getting smaller; big churches will keep attracting larger numbers of the already convinced (often at the expense of the smaller churches); the Christian population as a whole will remain in decline; and the *nones* will remain *nothing*."[13]

I have two precious grandchildren named Liv and Roman. They have their Pop wrapped around their fingers. It's amazing how much love God puts in our hearts for our grands. When I think about the world that Liv and Roman will experience, I feel both joy and pain. On one hand, they are surrounded by love and security. Faith in God runs deep on all sides of their immediate and extended family. That has been intentional, and they will reap its fruit. But on the other hand, they will be met by a culture steeped in darkness, where virtue and holiness are slipping toward none. What will become of the sanctity of life? Will there be none? What about the sanctity of marriage? Could there be none? How about a healthy fear for a holy God? Will it be none? Why should we expect less? This is the natural trajectory of a culture that is increasingly defining its faith as none, and a church that seems to be more comfortable making excuses than making disciples.

The question remains. Do we want to be healed? I pray that we do. There is a mighty Healer in our midst.

## A Mighty Healer Is in Our Midst

As the sick man by the Pool of Bethesda began giving a litany of excuses, it's as if Jesus didn't hear. Jesus simply said, "Get up, take up your bed, and walk" (John 5:8). There was only one thing he had to do to be healed. He had to obey, to just simply obey. Could it be that easy? No stirring of the waters? No elaborate pool diving program? The Bible says, "At once the man was healed, and he took up his bed and walked" (John 5:9).

Like the sick man, churches today have a litany of excuses for the condition they are in. If only our community was growing and there were not so many other churches surrounding us. If only we were in a better location and our people would give more, serve more, and pray more. The list goes on.

What we need is revival, but we keep looking for some mysterious moving of the waters. To this, Jesus simply says, "Get up, take up your cross, and go make disciples." There is only one thing we have to do. We must obey. It is that simple.

However, the question remains, do we want to be healed? Healing will require action.

First, we must repent of our spiritual narcissism. Narcissus is the figure in Greek mythology who fell in love with his own image reflected in a pool of water. Even the lovely nymph Echo could not lure him away from his self-absorption. Today the term narcissism refers to an exaggerated preoccupation with one's self. A narcissist is one who thinks, "It's all about me." Spiritual narcissism is killing the modern church.

If he or she were honest, the typical "church shopper" today would admit something like this: "I want to find a church that will feed me without offending me or expecting too much from me. I'm looking for one that will meet my needs, sing my music, love my kids, enrich my marriage, and do it in less than an hour each week because that is all the time I have to give." If your church is fortunate enough to be chosen by this consumer, you better not drop the ball. If you begin to grade too low in these areas, "the Lord will lead" this wonderful member to the church down the road that grades higher on the scorecard.

Not too long ago, an old friend stopped by my office. He came to inform me how "the Lord was leading." I had great respect for him, and earlier, I had invited him to join my D-Group on more than one occasion. As an older believer, I felt he had much to offer and could be trained to lead his own group. I love to equip older believers for multi-generation discipleship, but he never had the time to participate in our group. Instead, he had come to inform me that the Lord was leading him to the church down the road. He explained how much he loved to sing the old hymns. On his scorecard, the church down the road had a higher grade in this than we did.

Every pastor in America deals with issues like this weekly. Spiritual narcissism is real. How can we reach the nones when hymn-singing is more important than disciple-making?

I'm not against hymn singing, but let's be wise. If your church sits in a retirement community, you may want to sing older songs. If your church is surrounded by younger families, you might want to consider newer songs. Think about it. Even the old hymns were contemporary back in their day, and I'll bet some spiritual narcissists complained about them back then. Every new era will write new worship songs, and throughout history, there has been a link between singing new songs and reaching the next generation. As pastor J. D. Greer said in his message to the 2019 Southern Baptist Convention, "The church must decide if we love our traditions or love our grandchildren." If the church really wants to be healed, it must decide that it's not all about us. We must repent of spiritual narcissism.

Second, we must revitalize our discipleship strategies. I think Christians love programmed discipleship because it is convenient. All you have to do is show up. You go to an air-conditioned room, sit in a padded chair, visit with your close friends, and listen to a gifted teacher. Your children are cared for, refreshments are served, and homework is encouraged but not required. The only thing expected of you is to keep showing up and to sign up for the next class. Spiritual growth is guaranteed, and you're assured to grow deep in God's Word. Right? But how many lost and unchurched people are we reaching in our discipleship classes? Usually none. The nones are not looking for a good Bible class to attend. This was an effective strategy back when most Americans were looking for a church to attend, but those days have long passed. Even back then, this is not what Jesus modeled or mandated. His strategy calls for us to be disciple-making people. The problem is His call is not convenient. It calls for sacrifice. It involves taking up a cross and dying to self. It's not about sitting in padded chairs but going to broken people. It's not about hanging out with your friends, but it calls for reaching out to strangers.

Here is a painful truth. We like to talk about making disciples until it comes to the point of actually doing it. When challenged in this area, many will say, "We just don't have time for that." To be fair, we must make sure that the demands of our many programs are not poaching the time and energy required for our mission. The temptation we face is to cherish our programs more than we value our mission.

After all, don't we have some examples of churches around us that are growing because of their excellent discipleship programs and entertaining worship services? Some think all we have to do to reach the masses is to dress casual, provide free coffee, sing contemporary songs, and share twenty-minute feel-good messages. Throw in a giant video wall and a hipster band with skinny jeans, cool hair, and tattoos and your church is guaranteed to grow. If you top this off with a variety of small groups meeting for discipleship, then you are set to become the next megachurch.

Many believe this is true. They may even point out the new multisite church down the road that has exploded with growth by doing these very things. However, James White cautions us to take a closer look at those churches. He states, "How much of their growth is transfer growth and how much is truly conversion growth? And even if they claim a high number of baptisms, who are they baptizing? In many cases, even the baptism numbers are those rededicating their life (rebaptisms) or Presbyterians getting dunked as adults."[14]

We must understand the difference between discipleship and disciple-making. When most churches today talk about "discipleship," they are mainly referring to Bible studies. Their discipleship program consists of small groups that meet to study the Bible or to fellowship around a common interest. Certainly, there is nothing wrong with a good Bible study. However, many have been attending Bible studies for years who never feel compelled to carry out the mandate of the Great Commission. They participate in a small-group study and want to know when the next one is and the next one and the next one. We are making Bible learners but not disciple makers. The Great Commission was no call to join a discipleship program but an invitation to a lifestyle of disciple-making. We are called to make disciples who make disciples who make disciples. Our purpose is not to build a big church through transfer growth but to build God's kingdom on earth through the greater work of making true disciples.

In truth, there are no quick fixes or clever gimmicks that will produce true kingdom growth. There is no magic stirring of the water. As we saw in our friend by the Pool of Bethesda, the key is found in obedience. Simple obedience to Christ and His Great Commission is the ultimate key to revival in today's church. This means so much more than going on occasional mission trips or giving to mission causes. It means to intentionally make disciples who make disciples.

What is the church anyway? People often say, "I go to church." This statement can be misleading. By this, they usually mean that they are going to a building to attend a religious service. In truth, no one goes to church. We are the church.

The Greek word for church is *ekklesia*. It is used 114 times in the New Testament and most often refers to a local body of believers. The word is derived from the preposition *ek*, meaning "out of," and the verb *kaleo*, meaning "to call." It means "to call out" or "the called-out ones." As followers of Christ, what specifically are we are called out to do? The answer is easy. We are not called out to attend religious services, but to go make disciples.

We see this in the early church. First and foremost, the early church was a disciple-making movement. They were regular people who met anytime and anywhere for the purpose to make and multiply disciples. As the Lord added daily those who were being saved, they would find a place to gather for baptism, communion, and to celebrate the greater work that God was doing among them. They would come together to worship the Lord, listen to the apostles' teaching, and spend time in prayer so that they could become better disciple-makers. Everything they did was for the greater work.

We can experience this movement once again. The church in America can be healed. The Mighty Healer is in our midst if we really want to be healed.

I have hope that we do and let me tell you why. It's my friend Wirt, like dirt. He gives me hope. I see in Wirt and many others like him a renewed hunger for the greater work. I'm truly encouraged by the many, everyday believers who have a passionate desire to become disciples who make disciples. As John Dickerson says, "Christ calls each of us to 'go and make disciples.' Our greatest potential for reaching the lost is not a celebrity leader, but millions of less-known everyday believers."[15]

To intentionally build a disciple-making culture in our churches, it is vital for us to diligently equip these "less-known believers" for the greater work. In many churches, this is the missing link.

## 🔍 Discussion Questions For A Small Group Study

1. What big question did the author suggest that today's church must answer and why? How do you honestly think most in the church would answer this question? What are some indicators that the church in America is not well and needs revival?

2. What is the fastest-growing religious group in America today and who are these people? Why are recent headlines about America's booming megachurches misleading in terms of the true condition of the church? In your church, do you see more transfer growth or conversion growth and why do you think this is?

3. What is spiritual narcissism? In what ways is the cancer of narcissism killing the modern church? Why do some people like to talk about making disciples until it comes to the point of really doing it? What programs of your church might be poaching the time and energy required for your main mission?

4. What does the Greek word for "church" actually mean? How can it be misleading when someone says, "I go to church"? Instead of going to church, why is it more important to go as the church to carry out our Great Commission?

5. The Mighty Healer is in our midst, but what must today's church do to be healed? What do you think

it would take for the church to experience a vast disciple-making movement like that of the early church? Is there any area of spiritual narcissism that you need to confess and forsake today?

**Closing Prayer:** Oh, Father, we need revival in our church. Forgive us for our many excuses. Stir our hearts. Right now we pray for a grassroots disciple-making movement to begin to arise with us.

# CHAPTER 4

# The Missing Link

*And he went up on the mountain and called to him those whom he desired, and they came to him. And he appointed twelve (whom he also named apostles) so that they might be with him and he might send them out to preach and have authority to cast out demons.*
—Mark 3:13–15

Put on your big boy pants. You too, girls. Building a disciple-making culture in your church will not be easy. You will be working against years of tradition. Discipleship programs have been around for a long time. When you begin to make the transition from a program of discipleship to a disciple-making culture, don't think you won't encounter resistance. For most, it's all they've ever known. When you share new ideas about disciple-making, there will be those who remind you that "we've never done it that way before." Going out into the world to make disciples is far less convenient than coming into the church for a discipleship class. Some believers are not comfortable being inconvenienced for the gospel, and they might even "be led" to the church down the road. Are you ready for this?

Leading a church through this transition is always a struggle. Our adversary is a roaring lion, and he is always seeking a good church to devour. Times of change are opportune times for him to attack. Watch for him and be wise. It requires patience and perseverance to lead a church through a necessary season of transition.

Leading your church to build a disciple-making culture may be the most important thing you will ever do. You must be in it for the long haul. However, it's unlikely to come without pain. Some will question your motives and your intentions. Leading change is not for sissies. Be strong and courageous, but also be humble and gentle. Know when to press the gas and when to back it off a little. Trust the Holy Spirit to guide your steps. When God gives you a vision, He will guide you in the execution of it.

## Seeing the Vision for a Disciple-Making Culture

I am blessed to pastor a great church. When I was called to be their pastor, their vision was to relocate the church campus to a forty-acre plot of land in Trussville, Alabama. The people had a mind to work and a heart for God, and the move to our new location went much smoother than anyone would have expected. We built the first phase of our building plan and moved our entire congregation to Trussville in November of 2002.

NorthPark Church was the exciting new church in the area and growth came easy at first. Attendance and giving soared. However, even though our baptisms were up, the majority of our growth was the result of transfer growth. Nevertheless, times were good and space was tight. We felt the need to move forward with the second phase of our building plan. What we didn't see coming was the economic crash of 2008. Almost immediately, the rapid growth in our community ceased while our church had taken on a heavy burden of new construction debt.

At the same time, we were no longer the new church in town as other churches moved in around us. You know where this is going, don't you? I'm beginning to sound like the man by the Pool of Bethesda—excuses, excuses. After a while, I grew weary of making excuses.

Like the pastors that Rondie and I spoke with at the Jacksonville Pastor's Conference, I couldn't honestly say that any ministry in our church was truly multiplying. We tried to multiply our Life Group (Sunday school) classes, but it was a struggle. Our classes didn't want to multiply. I began to diligently seek the Lord for answers.

How did Jesus make disciples who make disciples? This a question I couldn't get out of my mind. To find the answer I dove deep into the Bible. I launched into a study of the four Gospels, highlighting and taking copious notes on every single passage related to Jesus and His disciples. It was out of this study that God begin to birth a vision in my heart for a disciple-making culture.

This is the missing link for most ministries. How can you lead your church to transition to a disciple-making culture if you don't know what one looks like? I'm grateful for the education I received at Southwestern Baptist Theological Seminary. Most of this book was written from the library at SWBTS. I wouldn't be where I am today apart from the wonderful professors who invested in my life during my time there. However, as a seminary student, I learned how to lead a discipleship program but not how to build a disciple-making culture. I learned how to share my faith but not how to live a lifestyle of disciple-making.

The Bible says, "Where there is no prophetic vision the people cast off restraint, but blessed is he who keeps the law" (Proverbs 29:18). The first step toward building a disciple-making culture in your church is for God to give you a vision of one. When He does, it will be the purest vision of His church you've ever seen. Be prepared, your life and your ministry will never be the same.

The hardest part will be to step outside of the box that others have built about discipleship. You may have lived in this box for a very long time and, though it may be difficult, it's essential. You must get outside that box and let Jesus teach you about disciple-making with fresh eyes.

## Equipping Your People for a Disciple-Making Culture

The second step toward building a disciple-making culture in your church is for God to show you how to execute the vision. Thomas Edison is credited with saying, "Vision without execution is hallucination." But let's be clear, execution will be the hardest part. As stated previously, we all like to talk about making disciples until it comes to the point of actually doing it.

In the church that I pastor, we started with our church staff. I laid out a plan for each member of our staff to begin leading a D-Group. A D-Group is a small group of three to five people who meet weekly for intentional discipleship. Each D-Group leader is responsible to invite others into the group, which can meet anytime and anywhere. To build a disciple-making culture in your church, the pastor and other church leaders must lead by example.

The next step is to share the vision with the church. I did this through a Sunday morning message series entitled, "Living the D-Life." The big idea of the series was that "Disciple-making is not a program; it's a lifestyle." In this multi-week series, I shared that living the D-Life means living a lifestyle of disciple-making, and I unpacked the six practices of disciple-making that Jesus modeled for us in the Gospels.

After the sermon series, the next step was to equip new leaders to lead D-Groups from our congregation. To accomplish this, I developed a *D-Life Training Notebook* and started recruiting leaders to attend the training, which we called a D-Life Boot Camp. In our first D-Life Boot Camp, several new men and women were trained for a lifestyle of disciple-making and equipped to begin leading a D-Group. We continue to lead this training every year in our church.

It's humbling to see how God has used this training in our church and many others. After leading our first D-Life training event, my wife, Rondie, and I have traveled the country leading D-Life Boot Camps in many churches, associations, and state conventions. Thousands of people in churches across the US and several different countries have started using D-Life as a tool for making disciples who make disciples.

In the meantime, building a true disciple-making culture in our church at NorthPark is a work in progress. We press on toward the goal but have a long way to go. We haven't arrived, but we're making strides. Our goal is not just to train people to lead a D-Group while they are at our church, but to equip them to be disciple-makers for the rest of their lives. When someone is led away from our church, I encourage them to begin a D-Group wherever they end up. I often remind them: "You don't need permission to do the Great Commission."

A wonderful couple in our church went through D-Life Training and started leading a D-Group. I was sad when they told me they were moving to Atlanta to begin a new job. They were great church members and disciple-makers. I regretted losing their leadership in our church. However, even before they settled in on a church in Atlanta, they informed me that had already started a new D-Group. They got it! You don't need permission to do the Great Commission. Disciple-making is a lifestyle!

The vision of our church is to train thousands of men, women, and teenagers to be disciple-makers who are advancing God's kingdom on earth. We want to build an army of common people who lead D-Groups in homes, restaurants, coffee shops, cafés, schools, businesses, apartments, prisons, parks, and mission centers all over our city. We want to see D-Groups going outside the walls of our church every week for the purpose of ministry and evangelism. We want to see D-Groups continually multiplying as they make disciples who make disciples. This is what a disciple-making culture looks like, and this is what we are laboring to build.

## The Important Key to a Disciple-Making Culture

Simplicity is the key. If it's simple, it's reproducible. You can't build a disciple-making culture without a simple process to develop disciple-making people.

Jesus modeled simplicity. He called twelve men "so that they might be with him and he might send them out to preach" (Mark 3:14). He kept everything simple so that these common men could learn how to make disciples. If they could learn to do it, then anyone can.

From Jesus, we learn that disciple-making works best through the caring, relational environment of a small discipleship group or "D-Group." For us, a D-Group could be as small as three to five people who meet anytime and anywhere for the purpose of intentional discipleship. I know that Jesus had twelve in His group, but we are not Jesus. A group of no more than five or six is best for our success.

By reading the Gospels, we learn there are six practices of disciple-making that Jesus modeled for us with His D-Group: (1) fellowship, (2) teaching, (3) prayer, (4) ministry, (5) multiplication, and (6) accountability. For now, let's take a brief overview of these practices.

First, there was fellowship. Jesus called His disciples to come and have intimate fellowship with Him. Like Jesus, you must take the initiative to invite others to join you in a D-Group. D-Groups can meet anytime and anywhere. Meeting away from the church allows you to meet people on their turf and provides opportunities for more gospel conversations. Diversity in age and spiritual maturity can enhance the dynamics of your group.

Second, there was teaching. Jesus taught His disciples using stories and interactive group discussions. With the Bible as your only textbook, D-Groups should commit to daily Bible reading and to joining together weekly for an interactive Bible study.

Third, there was prayer. Jesus prayed with His disciples and taught them how to pray. Likewise, D-Groups should pray together and practice the discipline of prayer in their daily lives. A weekly priority of every D-Group should be to pray for revival and spiritual awakening in our land.

Fourth, there was ministry. Jesus did ministry with His disciples and sent them out for ministry and evangelism.

Genuine discipleship requires more than a classroom. Like Jesus and His disciples, we must go out and do ministry together. Ministering together as a D-Group is a vital part of discipleship. A minimum goal of every D-Group should be to participate together in at least one community ministry and evangelism project every two months.

Fifth, there was multiplication. Jesus trained His disciples to go out and make other disciples. A major goal of every D-Group is to multiply within one to two years. Remaining together until Jesus returns is not our purpose. The goal is multiplication. Apart from multiplication, there is no real discipleship.

Sixth, there was accountability. Jesus held His disciples accountable to these practices of disciple-making. Accountability is vital in a relational environment committed to genuine spiritual growth. Powerful transformation can and will occur through the loving accountability of D-Groups. Spiritual strongholds related to alcohol, drugs, pornography, sexual identity issues, and many others can be broken through loving spiritual accountability.

In John 13:15, Jesus said, "For I have given you an example, that you also should do just as I have done to you." It would be impossible for us to create a better disciple-making process than that of Jesus. It would be wise for us to follow His example and to do it just like Him.

## A Father, a Son, and a Zebco 33

As a child growing up in the small town of Piedmont, Alabama, I was blessed to have a great home and wonderful parents. People who knew that I was Durward Wilks' son would often say to me, "Your father is a good man." That always made me feel proud.

When I was seven years old, my dad said, "Son, I want to teach you how to fish." I was so excited. I knew my dad loved to fish, and I always wanted to do everything that he did. One day we loaded our fishing gear and headed out to my Uncle Bill's lake. It was a beautiful private lake just outside of town on my uncle's farm.

When we arrived, my dad told me there were a lot of fish in this lake and that we needed to catch them. But how? I was only seven; I didn't know how to fish.

Then my dad did something that was a game-changer. He placed in my hands a fishing rod and a reel. "This is a Zebco 33," he said, "It's the most simple and reliable fishing reel that you will ever use." With only a few tries, I could cast out the bait as I followed my dad's instructions.

That day my dad taught me how to fish with a Zebco 33. He is in heaven now, but thanks to my loving dad, I can still catch fish today.

What I'm glad my dad didn't do was to take me fishing without teaching me how. I wouldn't have known where to begin. I probably would have jumped in the water and begun swimming around looking for a fish to catch with my bare hands. It would have never happened. After many failed attempts, even a determined boy like me would be forced to give up. I would have left that day and concluded that fishing was just not my thing.

No loving father would do this. He would never take his son fishing and not teach him how to fish. Yet, this is exactly what we often do in our churches.

We preach regularly about the Great Commission and challenge our people to make disciples. But we fail to teach them how. We leave them to learn for themselves, and after many failed attempts, they eventually give up and conclude that disciple-making is just not their thing. They decide to leave fishing for men to the "professionals."

But what if we could put in their hands a tool—like a Zebco 33—that was for fishing for men? Then, we could give them a simple tool for disciple-making and teach them how to use it. This is the missing link.

As pastors and ministers, our main job is "to equip the saints for the work of ministry" (Ephesians 4:12). The greater work of ministry is to make disciples who make disciples. It is time for us to do our jobs and to train God's people for a lifestyle of disciple-making.

In the second part of this book, I want to help with this. We will turn our focus to actually "doing the greater work." These next chapters will provide a practical guide on how to live a lifestyle of disciple-making. Many books talk about disciple-making, but the goal of this book is to train you how.

## Discussion Questions for a Small Group Study

1. Why is leading a church through transition always a struggle? How are seasons of change opportune times for Satan to attack? Despite the challenges, why is leading your church to build a disciple-making culture one of the most important things you can ever do?

2. To build a disciple-making culture in your church, what did the author say was the "missing link" for most ministries? Why do you agree or disagree? Why

is the first step toward building a disciple-making culture the need for God to give you the vision of one? How did the author describe what a disciple-making culture looks like?

3. What exactly is a D-Group? Why does disciple-making work best through the caring, relational environment of a D-Group? How many people did the author recommend per group that was best for its success? Why do you agree or disagree? Where can a D-Group meet?

4. Why is "simplicity" an important key to disciple-making? What six practices of disciple-making did Jesus model for us with His D-Group? How would you briefly describe each of these six practices? Read John 13:15. Why is it wise for us to follow Jesus' example and to make disciples just like He did it?

5. Read Ephesians 4:12. According to this verse, what is one main job of pastors and ministers? Why is it essential for us to do our job and to equip God's people for a disciple-making movement?

**Closing Prayer:** Heavenly Father, give us a clear vision for a disciple-making culture in our church and grant us the courage to lead our church to build it.

# PART 2

# DOING THE GREATER WORK

# CHAPTER 5

# Talking To Strangers

## The Fellowship of D-Life

*He appointed the twelve: Simon (to whom he gave the name Peter); James the son of Zebedee and John the brother of James (to whom he gave the name Boanerges, that is, Sons of Thunder); Andrew, and Philip, and Bartholomew, and Matthew, and Thomas, and James the son of Alphaeus, and Thaddaeus, and Simon the Zealot, and Judas Iscariot, who betrayed him.*
—Mark 3:16–19

So, you want to be a disciple-maker? Okay, but where do you start and how do you do it?

First, let me applaud you. As a believer, your supreme purpose in life is to make disciples. Even above your profession or position in life, disciple-making is your greater work. Your desire to be a disciple-maker is a testimony of your love for Christ, and in reading this book, you've made the first step.

Second, let me say, "You can do it." Jesus called regular people to be disciple-makers, not just preachers, teachers, or the super-religious. If the twelve guys He called to be His first disciples could do it, then you can do it. After all, when He gave you your Great Commission, He promised to be with you. The Spirit of the greatest disciple-maker who ever lived lives in you. The DNA of disciple-making is in your blood. It flows through your veins.

Now let's get back to the question. Where do you start and how do you do it? The good news is that Jesus made it simple. He made it so simple that anyone can do it. This doesn't mean there won't be challenges. Disciple-making involves people, and people have challenges. However, the process of disciple-making is simple.

Jesus taught us that the best way to make disciples is through the caring, relational environment of a small discipleship group, or a D-Group. Jesus invited twelve men to be in His D-Group. However, as stated before, a group of no more than five or six is best for our success.

When you think about a D-Group, think of a small group that can meet anytime and anywhere for the purpose of intentional discipleship. Your group should plan to meet weekly and strive to be consistent.

Jesus modeled six practices of disciple-making. To make disciples like Him, you must follow these same practices with your group: (1) fellowship, (2) teaching, (3) prayer, (4) ministry, (5) multiplication, and (6) accountability. These six practices of D-Life will help you to develop a lifestyle of disciple-making.

In this chapter, we will begin by focusing on practice number one—the fellowship of D-Life. Intimate fellowship with others is the main priority in disciple-making. As Jesus began His public ministry, His first order of business was to call twelve men to come and live an intimate fellowship with

Him and with one another. He intentionally chose them to be in His D-Group.

Likewise, you cannot lead a D-Group unless you take the first step of inviting some people to come be in your group. Jesus has called you to be a "fisher of men." This involves more than merely announcing that you are starting a D-Group. You must "go fishing" for some men or women to join with you in your group, and you must keep on fishing until you catch some. Like every good fisherman, you must be patient and persistent in this.

Real disciple-making is not the same as merely plugging into a "discipleship program," where people simply show up, fill up chairs, and listen to a teacher. To begin a disciple group, you must go get some people and find a place to meet with them. The good news is that your group can meet anytime or anywhere. Homes, restaurants, coffee shops, cafés, schools, places of business, prisons, and mission centers are just a few good places to begin a D-Group. After all, to catch some fish, you've got to go where the fish are.

One more thing, real disciple-making is not the same as grabbing three or four of your close friends to form an "accountability group," read some good books, and stay together until Jesus comes back. I'm not sure what that is, but it's not disciple-making. It sounds more like a clique, and Jesus was not too fond of cliques.

One thing I love about leading a D-Group is the close relationships that I have built over the years with many different people. Some were people that I hardly knew until I asked them to join the group. It's amazing how close you become with others when you are in a discipling relationship with them. These friendships will last a lifetime.

Let's take a closer look at the example of Jesus and learn from Him how to begin a D-Group. In disciple-making, it's not about simply starting a group, but it's how you start it that matters.

## Choosing a D-Group Must Be Intentional

When I was young, I often went fishing with my dad. We had a lot of fun and caught a lot of fish together. However, in our days of fishing, there is one thing we never did. We never caught a fish by accident. Not one.

Likewise, you will never start a D-Group by accident. You must be intentional about fishing for people to be in your group. Fishing calls for patience and persistence. Fish don't always bite easily. You will cast your bait and bring it in empty more times than you will catch a fish, but good fishermen are not easily discouraged. They keep on fishing until they catch some. The good thing about starting a D-Group is that you only need two or three people to get started.

There are some important lessons to learn from Jesus about choosing your group. You must take these lessons to heart if you want to be an effective disciple-maker.

First and foremost, understand the importance of prayer. Jesus went up on a mountain to pray before He called His disciples. The Bible says, "In these days he went out to the mountain to pray, and all night he continued in prayer to God. And when day came, he called his disciples and chose from them twelve, whom he named apostles" (Luke 6:12-13). Jesus made choosing His D-Group a matter of fervent prayer. He spent an entire night praying for God to show Him whom He should invite to be in His group.

You don't need to ask God "if" He wants you to make disciples. Jesus has already commanded you to make disciples. The prayer you must pray is: "Lord, who? Who do you want me to ask to join in my D-Group?" This is a very important first step. Don't skip it. As you pray, Jesus may show you someone to ask that you may have never imagined.

Next, understand the impact of hospitality. In the New Testament, the Greek word for "hospitality" is *philozenia*. It comes from two Greek words—*philos*, meaning "affection" or "brotherly love" and *zenos*, meaning "stranger." Hospitality in the Bible means, "to show love to a stranger." The writer of Hebrews said, "Do not neglect to show hospitality to strangers" (Hebrews 13:2).

Talking to strangers is an essential requirement for making disciples. Since unbelievers today are less willing to come to our turf, we must learn to play on theirs. A key to this is practicing biblical hospitality. David Mathis, the executive editor for the website Desiring God, says that Christian hospitality involves "welcoming unbelievers into our space, in hopes of bringing Jesus into theirs."[16]

As someone who is committed to a life of disciple-making, practicing Christian hospitality will open closed doors for you. You will always be on the lookout for new people to disciple. Your life is built around a never-ending process of discipling a small group, multiplying some out, and finding someone new to disciple. This requires thinking ahead. By showing hospitality to a stranger today, it may open the door to invite him or her to join your D-Group tomorrow. Christian hospitality can become the open door for neighbors, classmates, work acquaintances, people you meet at the ballpark, and other public places to be those whom you have the joy of discipling and leading into a deeper relationship with Christ.

Finally, understand the initiative of leadership. After praying and showing genuine expressions of hospitality, you must take the initiative to act on God's leadership. Meet face-to-face with those whom God wants you to disciple and ask them to join in your group. Explain to them that D-Groups fellowship together weekly, read and discuss the Bible, and do ministry together. Don't be afraid to ask them to commit to the group. At this point, you are not inviting them to attend any church. You are simply inviting them to come hang out with you and some friends as you walk through the Bible together.

Many Christians are like the famous deputy sheriff we came to know and love from the golden age of television sitcoms. He was allowed to have only one bullet in his gun. Likewise, many Christians have only one bullet. From time to time, they invite someone to come visit their church. However, when those they invite say they go to another church, their one bullet has been used. Because they don't want to "proselyte" them, they feel they can't ask them again.

As a disciple-maker, you don't have just one bullet. Remember, you are not inviting people to come to your church. You are inviting them to come hang out with you. Let them know that your purpose is not to proselyte them, but to walk through the Bible with them. What you may discover is that they are not really active at another church but only attend during Easter and Christmas. These are people you should invite to come to your church. You may also discover that they have never been saved, and you can lead them to Christ. If they are active at another church, then don't proselyte them. Train them how to make disciples and multiply them out to lead their own D-Group. Most churches don't have a multiplying process of discipleship and you will be training a disciple-maker for them. Never assume that just because others tell you they go to church that they are genuine followers of Christ. Continue to encourage them to join in your D-Group until you know where they are in their spiritual lives.

Remember, fish don't always bite easily. Don't get discouraged when you cast out the bait and bring it back empty. You must keep casting out the bait to catch a fish.

Take a second to think about your current fishing holes. Where could you begin to start fishing for people for your D-Group? Your family, neighborhood, workplace, school, clubhouse, grocery store, ballpark, and so many other fishing holes are all around you, and that's not to mention your church. In your church, you can find other mature believers to help you lead your group and to be trained to multiply. You will also find new believers and struggling believers who need to be discipled. What about an existing ministry in your area that could use you to come alongside and offer assistance with discipleship?

Hoyt and Norm are two senior adults who participated in a D-Life training event that was held at our church. Hoyt was in his eighties and Norm in his seventies. After praying, they felt led to start a D-Group together at a community service center in Birmingham, Alabama, known as "Three Hots and a Cot." It's a home for veterans that offers three hot meals a day and a cot to sleep on. When Hoyt and Norm first went to the home, they were introduced as two preachers who were there to preach. Neither one of them is a preacher, but the announcement was enough to send veterans scurrying to their rooms. Not to be deterred, they went back the next week. The only one to welcome them was the Golden Retriever on the front porch. They went back the third week and one veteran named Clarence wanted to join them. After a few weeks of participating in the D-Group, Hoyt and Norm had the joy of leading him to faith in Christ. Unfortunately, Clarence had a major stroke shortly after his commitment to Christ and spent several weeks in the hospital. It appeared that he might not make it, but his new friends were praying for him.

After his recovery, it was on a wonderful Sunday morning that I had the privilege to baptize Clarence in our church at NorthPark. He believes to this day that the reason God allowed him to recover was so that he could be baptized. The first contact that Clarence had with our church was through Hoyt and Norm's D-Group that met at Three Hots and a Cot. Clarence went on to become a faithful member of our church and to help Hoyt and Norm start other D-Groups and lead other veterans to Christ. This is the power of disciple-making. It reminds me of the things we read about in the Book of Acts. Praise God for two senior adults who are making disciples and making a difference in their retirement years. We need more seniors like them.

I hope you are ready to begin making disciples and making a difference as well. Pray for God to guide you. Then take the initiative to choose a small group of people to disciple. A group of three to five is a great start. You may add a new disciple or two along the way. You should never turn anyone away. However, when your group grows to six or eight, you should multiply out a new group as soon as possible. You will not be able to effectively disciple more than five or six at a time.

## Connecting with Your D-Group Will Be Imperative

After choosing a small group to disciple, you must connect with them weekly. The Bible says that Jesus "appointed twelve . . . so that they might be with him" (Mark 3:14). He simply called them to "be with him." You cannot disciple others apart from intimate fellowship with them. Remember that you can meet anytime and anywhere. The important thing is that you meet regularly.

Job constraints may prohibit some from attending weekly. In such cases, encourage attendance as much as possible. Touch base with these individuals often to share prayer requests and to hold them accountable in their daily Bible reading.

During the summer months, do not shut down your group. If even one or two are available, meet with them. Even when you cannot meet, keep in touch with your group during the summer months and holiday seasons. Consistency is essential.

## Characteristics of Your D-Group Will Be Important

When you begin to pray about people to invite to join your D-Group, there are some important group characteristics to keep in mind. You only have so much time to give to your team and you want to invest your time wisely. Choose your group carefully.

First, you want a diverse group. One thing you notice about the group of disciples whom Jesus called is their diversity. His group included four fishermen, a government worker who collected taxes for Rome, and a political revolutionary who hated tax collectors, to name a few. When He first called them, we don't even know if they were true believers or not. Judas never did become a true believer and eventually betrayed

Him. Nevertheless, we learn from Jesus that diversity in our D-Groups is important. The more diversity you have in your group, the more dynamic it will be.

You want to have mature believers in your D-Group. You want to have at least one or two others who can help you lead the group, and who can be prepared to lead a new group when it's time to multiply. Since our goal is to multiply new D-Groups, you always want to have someone whom you are equipping to lead. It's also good to have someone who can lead the group when you must be away.

You also want to have new believers in your group. New believers are hungry for God's Word and eager to learn from mature believers. They add value and a great sense of purpose to your group. When a new believer immediately connects with a D-Group, it is one of the most effective ways for him or her to experience great spiritual growth.

It is also great to have unbelievers in your D-Group. Think outside the walls of your church. There are many lost and unchurched individuals who are seeking answers to life. They might be more than willing to join a small group meeting in a home or coffee shop where they can discuss the Bible and find fellowship. It's likely that a lost person will be led to faith in Christ and eventually connect with the church through the fellowship and witness of a D-Group.

In addition, you want to have a multigenerational group. In the Bible, Paul instructed his disciple Titus to be intentional about multigenerational discipleship. Paul said that the older men and women should intentionally disciple the younger men and women (Titus 2:1–11). Just as the early church practiced multigenerational discipleship, so must we. Senior adults are one of the greatest resources for disciple-making in the church today. We must intentionally involve them in our D-Groups. Strive for a multi-generational group.

In one of my first D-Groups, I had a young new believer and a retired pastor. I watched the bond between them grow. I was the leader of the group, but every time the retired pastor would speak, the new believer would lean in to hear every word. Multigenerational discipleship creates a beautiful and powerful atmosphere for spiritual growth.

Remember, the more diversity you have in your group, the more dynamic it will be. Work hard and be intentional in creating diversity in your D-Group.

You not only want a diverse group but also a defective group. The disciples whom Jesus called had issues. They had all kinds of issues such as anger, pride, fear, and doubt. Likewise, you want to disciple people who have issues. It's not hard to find people with issues. There are people all around you who are battling addiction, anger, pornography, depression, greed, and sexual identity issues. They need someone to come alongside them with prayer and loving spiritual accountability.

In many ways, we are all defective because we all have issues. It is through the caring, relational environment of a D-Group that we can grow to become more like Jesus. Radical transformation can and will occur through the loving accountability of biblical discipleship.

Finally, strive to have a dedicated group. When you look for people to disciple, you want to find people who will be committed. Again, you only have so much time to give to your D-Group, and you want to make a wise investment of your time. You must be highly committed to your group and you must expect the same from them. Encourage those in your group to let you know in advance when they will not be able to meet.

When someone is unexpectedly absent, contact him or her promptly. Make regular use of texts, emails, and phone calls to encourage dedication and commitment. Loving accountability is a vital key to building commitment. The first disciples left their fishing nets, their boats, and even their fathers to follow after Jesus (Mark 1:16–20). They were dedicated. Likewise, we must be dedicated disciple-makers. The rewards of our labor will be great.

You can do this. God uses people like you to do the greater work of disciple-making. Once you begin, your life will never be the same. I don't think you will ever be able to stop living the D-Life.

Linda is a regular person with a very kind and sweet spirit. She participated in the very first D-Life Boot Camp we hosted at our church because she wanted to be trained for a lifestyle of disciple-making. After the training, Linda was so excited. Being a woman of faith, she stepped out to lead a group and began to pray about whom she should ask. The Lord placed on her heart an unchurched neighbor. Her neighbor and a few other women joined Linda's D-Group. After a few weeks of meeting together, Linda's unchurched friend said to the group, "I don't have what you ladies have. Could you tell me how to be saved?" Linda shared the good news of Christ with her, and she put her faith in Him for salvation. Immediately afterward, she said, "I have two daughters at home that have never heard this. If I go to get them right now will you share this with them?" She went to get her daughters and quickly brought them to Linda's house to hear the gospel. That night, both of her daughters also put their faith in Christ. A few weeks later, I had the joy of baptizing all three of them at our church. The very first contact they had with our church was in the home of a disciple-maker named Linda. This is the power of disciple-making.

God can use you in the same way. You can do it! I encourage you to step out in faith like Linda and begin leading a D-Group. Remember, you don't need permission to do the Great Commission.

## 🔍 Discussion Questions for a Small Group Study

1. According to the author, how is "real disciple-making" different from merely plugging into a "discipleship program?" How is "real disciple-making" different from merely grabbing three or four of your best friends and forming an "accountability group?" Why must choosing a D-Group be intentional?

2. In choosing a D-Group, what is of first importance and how did Jesus model this? What does it mean to practice true Christian hospitality and what role does this play in choosing a D-Group? Where are your current fishing holes to start fishing for people to be in your D-Group?

3. Why is it important to have diversity in your D-Group? Why would you want to have other mature believers in your group? Why would you want to have new believers in your group? Why would you want to have unbelievers in your group? Read Titus 2:1-11. What does the Bible say about multigenerational discipleship?

4. Why would you want to disciple people who have issues? What kind of issues did Jesus' disciples struggle with? What kind of issues do people around you struggle with today? How can radical transformation

occur through the loving accountability that can be provided by a D-Group?

5. When leading a D-Group, why must you be highly committed to your group and why must you expect the same from them? In what practical ways can you encourage others dedication to the group? Read Mark 1:16-20. How dedicated were the first disciples to their D-Group? Likewise, why must we be dedicated as disciple-makers?

**Closing Prayer:** Father, thank you for the example of Jesus in teaching me to be a disciple-maker. As I think about starting a discipleship group, please begin to show me who I should ask to be in my group. I thank you in advance for those you will give me the privilege to disciple.

# CHAPTER 6

# The Disciple-Makers Textbook

## *The Teaching of D-Life*

*Again he began to teach beside the sea. And a very large crowd gathered about him, so that he got into a boat and sat in it on the sea, and the whole crowd was beside the sea on the land. And he was teaching them many things in parables. . . . And when he was alone, those around him with the twelve asked him about the parables.*
—Mark 4:1–2, 10

So, you want to be a disciple-maker but you don't think that you're a teacher. Teaching is not your gift, and you don't like speaking in front of people. You would rather pet a spider than give a speech.

Well, you're in good shape. Disciple-making is not about giving speeches. The gift of teaching is not required. The word disciple means "a learner," and there are many different ways for a person to learn.

My friend Keith is a quiet man. By nature, he's an introvert. He is a good man who loves the Lord, his family, and his church. However, in a room full of strangers, you probably wouldn't know he was there. After going through D-Life training, Keith felt led to start a D-Group. Could a reserved man like Keith lead a D-Group? You bet he could. A big part of D-Life training is to help people like Keith believe that they can make disciples. It's not hard to train others to be disciple-makers once they believe they can do it. In a short time after completing D-Life training, Keith started a group at his workplace and led one of his coworkers to Christ. This is the power of disciple-making.

I suspect there were a few introverts among Jesus' twelve disciples, and I'm sure some of them didn't have the gift of teaching either. If we limit disciple-making to only those who are gifted teachers, how will common people live out their supreme purpose in life? That would limit the greater work to only a select few, which is precisely where we are in the church today.

This brings us back to the word "simple." Jesus modeled a simple method of teaching with His disciples. Mainly, He told stories. He would tell a simple story or parable, and when He was alone with His disciples, they would discuss the story. By keeping it simple, He made it reproducible. Anyone can learn to teach like Jesus by telling stories.

So, where do we find these stories that Jesus told? We find them in the Bible. The Bible is the disciple-makers textbook. It's the only resource we need to make disciples who make disciples. By leading your group to read the Bible, story through the Bible, and discuss the Bible, you can teach in the same way that Jesus taught His disciples.

## Lead Your Group to Read the Bible

In true disciple-making, the Bible should be our only textbook. As stated earlier, we only have so much time to give to our D-Group. We must use our time wisely. In making disciples, why would you want to use any other book except The Book—The Holy Bible? Some use other people's books to study with their discipleship groups. I don't know why you would do this. I love reading books by great Christian authors, theologians, and apologists, but I can read those on my own time. Those books may be great resources for a small group study, but not for disciple-making.

The Bible is the only book that is "living and active, sharper than any two-edged sword, piercing to the division of soul and of spirit, of joints and marrow, and discerning the thoughts and intentions of the heart" (Hebrews 4:12). It's the only book that is "breathed out by God and profitable for teaching, for reproof, for correction, and for training in righteousness, that the man of God may be complete, equipped for every good work" (2 Timothy 3:16-17). The Bible is "more to be desired . . . than gold, even much fine gold" (Psalm 19:10). Why would you use someone else's book when you can use the Bible?

Often, it's because of laziness. Other people's books may seem more entertaining or easier to read. Because of this, there are not many believers who read the Bible regularly. This is a big reason for the spiritual shallowness that we see in the church today. However, when you read the Bible, it is transformational. This is why you must lead people to read the Bible.

I concur with Donald Whitney in his classic work, *Spiritual Disciplines for the Christian Life*, where he says, "No Spiritual Discipline is more important than the intake of God's Word. Nothing can substitute for it. There simply is no healthy Christian life apart from a diet of the milk and meat of Scripture."[17] This is truth. There is no substitute for daily Bible reading.

As a D-Group leader, you must trust the total sufficiency of the Scriptures. Let the Holy Scriptures do the teaching for you. You don't have to be a great teacher. The Bible is the great teacher. Lead your group to systematically read and discuss the Bible and watch them grow.

Daily Bible reading is the single most life-changing thing that a believer can do. As a disciple-maker, leading others to develop the spiritual discipline of daily Bible reading is your priority. It's important to give your D-Group a Bible reading plan that is achievable. Setting unrealistic goals for your group is counterproductive. Think about how many believers have tried and failed to read through the entire Bible in a year. It's extremely challenging, especially if you fall behind.

I encourage you to begin by giving your group the realistic goal of reading through the New Testament together in one year. This can be accomplished by simply reading one chapter a day, five days a week. By holding one another accountable to this goal, you will read through the entire New Testament in exactly fifty-two weeks. By slowing down and reading only one chapter a day, you can meditate on each chapter and find personal application points for your daily life. This goal is simple, and there is no excuse for anyone not to achieve it. Other reading plans may involve reading the great stories of the Old Testament or reading through Psalms, Proverbs, and Ecclesiastes. The important thing is to give your group an achievable reading plan.

## Lead Your Group to Apply the Bible

Note keeping or journaling is another important spiritual discipline to lead your group to develop. Some believers like to do extensive journaling. However, I encourage you to keep your goals simple. Teach your group to find one personal application point from each chapter of the Bible by using the

SPACE acrostic. These five simple questions will help you and those in your group to make SPACE in your hearts for God's Word. In each chapter that you read, ask if there is a:

- Sin to confess
- Promise to claim
- Attitude to change
- Command to obey
- Example to follow

You will find an answer to at least one of these questions in every chapter of the Bible. Don't try to answer all five questions from each chapter but look for the one that jumps off the page at you. As the Holy Spirit leads you to the one that is for you, write it down. When the God of the universe speaks to you from His Word, you should always write it down.

Take time each week to let your group share some of their application points. This will be one of the most fruitful times in your D-Group meetings. These are things that the Holy Spirit has revealed to you from God's Word. Don't rush through this. Spend time discussing these points together.

Personal accountability is essential to help your group develop the spiritual disciplines of daily Bible reading and note keeping. It is often said that people don't do what they are supposed to do, they do what they are held accountable to do. Therefore, you will want to ask your D-Group two accountability questions every week:

- Did everyone read your daily Bible reading assignments?
- What are some of the application points that you found?

Asking these two questions will give you valuable insight into how each one in your group is growing and allow you to provide ongoing encouragement to those who are struggling. As redundant as it may seem, it will be important to ask the two accountability questions every week.

A man connected with a D-Group who had been away from God for quite some time said, after a couple of months of participating in the group, "I've read more Bible in the last six weeks than I have in my entire life." Accountability works!

## Lead Your Group to Memorize the Bible

Scripture memory is an important spiritual discipline for a disciple of Christ. The Psalmist said, "I have stored up your word in my heart, that I might not sin against you" (Psalm 119:11).

Jesus memorized Scripture. He quoted often from the Old Testament in His teaching and used Scripture to ward off the temptation of Satan in the wilderness. The early apostles memorized Scripture and quoted it often as they witnessed to others and as they defended their faith. By memorizing Scripture, you will have a valuable tool in hand to assist you in witnessing, counseling, and resisting temptation.

Lead your D-Group to memorize selected Scriptures that come out of your weekly Bible reading plan. Get them to memorize Scriptures from the Bible translation that they normally use. Instruct them to write out the weekly memory verse on an index card or small sheet of paper. Encourage them to go over the verse several times a day, committing each part of it to memory and to always give the chapter and verse reference. Allow your group to quote the verse out loud at your weekly D-Group meeting.

## Lead Your Group to Story Through the Bible

The Bible tells us that Jesus taught "many things in parables" (Mark 4:2). A parable is an earthly story that has a spiritual meaning. Storytelling was Jesus' main form of teaching with His disciples.

You can follow His example by storying through the Bible with your D-Group. Each week choose a different Bible story or important passage from your weekly reading plan for your group to discuss.

Make weekly assignments to get everyone in your group involved. Assign a different person each week to come prepared to briefly tell the story or paraphrase the passage. Assign another person to come prepared to read it from the Bible. These weekly assignments are a great way to encourage group participation and to equip those in your group for future leadership.

## Lead Your Group to Discuss the Bible

The Bible says that when Jesus was alone with His disciples, "the twelve asked him about the parables" (Mark 4:10). In these intimate moments, Jesus and His disciples would discuss His parables and unwrap the meanings of His teachings.

Likewise, involve your D-Group in a guided group discussion of the Bible story or key passage you have chosen to cover for the week. Facilitate the discussion by asking important questions about the story, which will help your group understand what the Bible is teaching and how it can be applied to their lives. Always remember that a facilitator does not lecture but simply leads the group in a guided discussion.

It will be essential for you to be a good role model as a facilitator. Your goal is to make disciples who make disciples, and it is important to always train those in your group how to lead. Begin assigning others to facilitate the discussion after a few weeks. Be sure to coach and encourage them as you prepare them for leadership.

Here are a few things to keep in mind as you facilitate the Bible study:

- Get everyone involved. Some in the group will be eager to jump into the discussion. For those who are timid, ask them specifically what they think about a particular discussion question.
- Stop someone from dominating the discussion. For those who are more talkative, ask them specifically to let someone else answer a particular question. If the problem persists, you may need to meet privately with this person to share the importance of giving everyone time to share in the discussion. You must lovingly and frankly address this issue. To fail to do so will jeopardize your group.
- Keep the discussion on point. In group discussions, it is not uncommon to get sidetracked. You will want to bring the focus of the group back to the question being discussed.
- Always be truthful, positive, and transparent. There will be times when someone in the group may share ideas contrary to sound Bible doctrine. Stay positive, avoid arguments, and affirm the individual's openness to share his or her view. But above all, be truthful and clear about your own biblical interpretation and convictions.

- Be sensitive to the Holy Spirit. As a D-Group grows closer together, some in the group will become more open to sharing personal struggles and challenges. Be sensitive to the leadership of the Holy Spirit in dealing with these situations. At times, it will be appropriate to stop and pray immediately for a group member and to take extra time to minister to his or her need. Always be CONFIDENTIAL with personal issues that are shared in your group.
- Be sure to close out every D-Group meeting with prayer. Pray specifically for the group to apply the truths learned in each week's Bible study.

## Lead Your Group to Prepare to Multiply

Always remember that your ultimate goal as a D-Group leader is to make disciples who make disciples. To multiply out a new D-Group must be a big priority. Prepare your group to multiply by equipping others in your group to lead. You can accomplish this by assigning specific leadership roles to different members of your group every week.

Begin by assigning someone to lead the group in prayer. After a brief time of fellowship, ask for prayer requests and have someone who is assigned to pray over the requests and for spiritual revival in our land.

Next, assign someone to tell the weekly Bible story or to paraphrase the passage. Encourage the storyteller to be brief and to simply tell the story or paraphrase the passage in one's own words. Even new believers can be involved in telling the story.

Assign someone to read the Bible story. After telling the story, have someone read it from the Bible to see if anything was left out.

Continue by assigning someone to facilitate the discussion. You will want to model this for the first few weeks and then begin assigning the role to others in the group.

These four weekly assignments are very important. By rotating these assignments, you not only get everyone in the group involved, but every week you are preparing them for multiplication and for leading a new D-Group. When you have less than four in your group, simply double up on an assignment.

As the D-Group leader, there will be weeks when your only job is to ask the two accountability questions. This is a good thing. Always keep in mind that your goal is to prepare your group to multiply. Your D-Group weekly agenda should look like this:

- Fellowship Time
- Prayer Time (Assignment 1: Someone will lead the group in prayer.)
- Accountability Time (Ask the two questions and share application points.)
- Story Time (Assignment 2: Someone will tell the story.)
- Bible Reading (Assignment 3: Someone will read the passage.)
- Bible Study (Assignment 4: Someone will facilitate the discussion.)
- Ministry Planning (We will discuss this in chapter 8.)
- Weekly Assignments (Make the four assignments for next week.)
- Closing Prayer

Let me encourage you to not let this chapter overwhelm you. You can do this. Remember to let the Bible do the teaching for you. You don't have to be a great communicator to lead a D-Group. The Bible is the great teacher. If you will lead your group to systematically read and discuss the Bible, you will see spiritual growth.

A few years ago, Scott came to our church, and I had the joy of leading him to Christ. He was raised by a Catholic family but had not been to church since he was a teenager. He knew very little about the Bible. I helped Scott connect with a D-Group, and he immediately began reading the Bible daily and discussing it with others in his group. I don't think I've seen a new believer grow in faith as quickly as Scott. As a result, God restored his relationship with his son and his family. Scott had a brother-in-law who came from another community to participate in one of our D-Groups because of the transformation he had seen in him. He said to the group, "This stuff really works! I've never seen a person whose life has been changed as much as my brother-in-law, Scott."

Yes, it works! It works because it's what Jesus taught us to do. It's a process that cannot fail.

## Lead Your Group To Use The D-Life Tool

To lead a group effectively, D-Group leaders often need a good track to run on and a simple tool to keep them on track. We have you covered on this.

D-Life Online or the *D-Life Journal* provides four full years of Bible reading plans, Scripture memory verses, and weekly study guides for your group. The *D-Life Weekly Study Guide* will provide everyone in your group with daily Bible reading assignments and a place to record personal application points and prayer requests. There is also a weekly Bible story for your group to discuss with several questions provided to help you facilitate a meaningful group discussion.

My wife and I have led D-Life Boot Camps for many churches, ministries, and associations across the country. D-Life Boot Camps provide four hours of intense training for living a lifestyle of disciple-making using the D-Life tool. We would love to come and lead D-Life training for your ministry.

For more information on D-Life training or to purchase D-Life Online or the *D-Life Journal*, go to: www.livethedlife .com. To view samples of these materials, see appendixes 1 and 2.

## ⌕ Discussion Questions for a Small Group Study

1. According to the author, why should the Bible be our only textbook in true disciple-making? Why do you think that most believers don't practice the spiritual discipline of daily Bible reading? Can you have a healthy Christian life apart from a steady diet of the milk and meat of God's Word? Why or why not?

2. Why is it important for you to set realistic goals as you strive to read the Bible daily? How can personal accountability help you with this? According to the author, what five questions can help you make SPACE in your heart for God's Word by finding personal application points from each chapter of the Bible?

3. Read Psalm 119:11. Why is it important to memorize the Bible? What practical tips can assist you in memorizing the Scriptures? How can Scripture memory help you in witnessing? How can it help you

in counseling others? How can it help you in resisting temptation?

4. What is a parable? Why do you think Jesus often taught His disciples by using parables? How can anyone learn to teach like Jesus by using the stories of the Bible? What makes a group discussion a highly effective method of teaching? What practical tips did the author give for facilitating a healthy discussion of the Bible?

5. In a D-Group, how can you prepare your group for multiplication by rotating weekly assignments? What four weekly assignments did the author suggest for you to make to different members of the group? Why is reading, applying, memorizing, and discussing the Bible a disciple-making process that cannot fail?

**Closing Prayer:** Heavenly Father, help me to be consistent in reading my Bible daily that I may grow as a disciple. I also pray that you will grant me the opportunity to help others develop this important spiritual discipline.

# CHAPTER 7

# Thy Kingdom Come

## *The Prayer of D-Life*

*Pray then like this:*
*"Our Father in heaven,*
*hallowed be your name.*
*Your kingdom come,*
*your will be done,*
*on earth as it is in heaven.*
*Give us this day our daily bread,*
*and forgive us our debts,*
*as we also have forgiven our debtors.*
*And lead us not into temptation,*
*but deliver us from evil."*
—Matthew 6:9–13

It would be hard to think of anything in life more needed than the power of fervent prayer. If there were ever a time when every believer in Christ should pray passionately and fervently, that time is now. We need a great movement of God to bring revival to the church, and prayer is essential to this. Unfortunately, the great power of prayer is often neglected.

As a disciple-maker, you must lead your D-Group to pray together and to practice the spiritual discipline of prayer in their daily lives. This is a very important part of disciple-making.

Jesus taught His disciples to pray. In Matthew 6:9-13, He gave them a model prayer that we often refer to as "The Lord's Prayer." He gave this prayer in response to one of His disciples who said to Him, "Lord, teach us to pray" (Luke 11:1).

The reason many believers don't know how to pray is that they have never been discipled in the discipline of prayer. The best way for us to learn to pray is by praying with others who are more mature in faith.

Great things happen when God's people join together in prayer. The late evangelist Ron Dunn said, "Prayer is the secret weapon of the kingdom of God. It is like a missile that can be fired toward any spot on earth, travel undetected at the speed of thought, and hit its target every time."[18]

## Teach Your Group the Priority of Prayer

As a D-Group leader, you should never meet with your group and not pray. Prayer should take priority over other things. No matter where you meet, you must pray, even in public places. By making prayer a priority in your D-Group, you are leading your group to make it a priority in their daily lives.

As your group comes together, grab some coffee and spend a few minutes in fellowship together. A great way to transition away from your fellowship time is to ask your group to share prayer requests.

Don't rush this. This is often when someone will open up and let you in, especially those who have been in the group for a while. When trust is built, he or she may take off the mask and reveal the fears, hurts, addictions, struggles, and weaknesses that might not be shared with anyone else. This will be a breakthrough moment and you must handle it carefully. Take time to listen. Spend extra time in sincere prayer over the matter. As the leader, you should follow up with this person during the week, express appreciation for the transparency shown, and pray over the matter again. These are special moments of discipleship and one reason why a group of no more than three to five is best. Such openness is unlikely to occur in a larger group. Remember that openness calls for strict confidentiality. If you violate a person's trust, he or she will never open up again.

As prayer requests are shared, encourage your group to write them down and to continue to pray over the requests during the week. The person that you have assigned to pray should lift up these specific requests in prayer each week.

If your group meets in a public place, it is not uncommon for others to be watching and listening. Though you must never pray for show, you must not be ashamed of your faith either. You may be surprised at the ministry opportunities this may open for you.

Rondie was meeting with her D-Group at a local café. An employee from the café had taken a table near them to attend to some work. Though she appeared to be preoccupied with her work, she was really listening. As Rondie was about to wrap up their meeting, the lady came over to the table. She confessed that she was listening in on their conversations and that it was just what she needed to hear. She was going through a difficult time in her life, and the Bible story they were discussing spoke directly to her needs. She apologized for listening in but spoke of how encouraging it was for her. Tears flowed as my wife and her group prayed over her right there in the café.

I hear stories like this regularly from disciple makers around the country. The Holy Spirit is the author of divine appointments. Keep your eyes open for them. They will be peak opportunities for ministry and will lead to many gospel conversations.

## Model for Your Group the Practice of Prayer

How does a new or spiritually immature believer learn to pray? Certainly, one could read some good books about prayer, however, the best way to learn to pray is by praying with other believers. Listening to the prayers of those who are more mature in their faith will nurture the practice of prayer in those less mature.

The Lord's Prayer is a model prayer and an example for us to follow. It was not given for us to memorize and repeat. It was given as an example of how we should pray. In this prayer, there is adoration, confession, thanksgiving, and supplication. These are the elements of a mature prayer. In leading a D-Group, you and other seasoned believers in the group should model praying a mature prayer.

The ACTS acrostic is a helpful tool to help you remember the elements of a mature prayer, which includes:

- Adoration—Praising God for who He is.
- Confession—Confessing your sins to God.
- Thanksgiving—Thanking God for the great things He has done.
- Supplication—Interceding for others and lifting up personal requests.

In your D-Group, be sure to include all these elements of a mature prayer when you pray over your weekly requests.

You will likely have someone in your group who has never prayed out loud with others and doesn't feel comfortable doing so. Be patient with this. Perhaps he or she can tell the Bible story or read the text, but there is no reason to assign one to pray who is not ready. Give it time. In a few months of praying with others, this one who has never prayed out loud may volunteer to pray. This is a great breakthrough in discipleship. He or she might be petrified but is likely to pray a most humble, beautiful, and sincere prayer. It may not be a mature prayer yet, but it will be real. Everyone in the group should affirm this new prayer warrior in the making.

## Nurture in Your Group Faith in Prayer

I love the story in the Bible where a group of early disciples gathered in a home to pray for Peter's release from prison. Peter had been seized by King Herod for preaching the gospel. He was locked up in prison and was being guarded by four squads of soldiers. Herod had bad intentions. He desired to kill Peter after the Passover. The outlook seemed hopeless for Peter, "but earnest prayer for him was made to God by the church" (Acts 12:5).

Indeed, prayer is the secret weapon of the kingdom of God. As the church was praying, an angel of the Lord was sent to deliver Peter from prison. The chains miraculously fell off his hands, the gate leading to the city opened of its own accord, and Peter was set free.

The humorous part of the story happened when Peter arrived at the house where the church was praying. When he knocked on the door of the house, a servant girl named Rhoda answered. Recognizing Peter's voice, she returned to the prayer meeting with joy to announce his arrival. You would think there would be a great celebration, but not with this group of mighty prayer warriors. They told Rhoda she was out of her mind, and they left Peter standing at the door. Peter was released from the prison cell but couldn't get into the prayer meeting.

As soon as I start to chuckle at this story, I come under conviction. I picture myself in that room, chastising a poor servant girl for interrupting my prayer time with her false hope. It was false hope, wasn't it?

Well, this group certainly thought so. That is until they finally let Peter in. How often are we just like them? Perhaps, they have one up on us. They at least had the faith to come together to pray.

As a D-Group leader, you must nurture faith in the power of prayer. This may be a stretch for you, as it is for me. I often feel like the man who prayed, "I believe; help my unbelief" (Mark 9:24)!

The more I pray with my D-Group, the more my faith has grown. Faith nurtures faith. The more answers to prayer I see, the more I begin to believe that prayer is the secret weapon of the kingdom of God. I believe that no situation is hopeless, chains can be broken, doors can miraculously open, and people can be set free.

Sometimes the darkness in our land is overwhelming. Is there any real hope for revival in our land? In the Lord's Prayer, the first actual request is, "Thy kingdom come" (Matthew 6:10). Jesus taught us to pray, "Thy kingdom come." That petition is a request for revival. As God's kingdom advances through His church, His will is done on earth as it is in heaven. Ultimately, this request is for Christ's return, but until His return, I long to see a revival on earth. If Jesus taught us to pray for revival, then there is hope.

In the Bible, God gave us a great promise to claim. He said, "If my people who are called by my name humble themselves, and pray and seek my face and turn from their wicked ways, then I will hear from heaven and will forgive their sin and heal their land" (2 Chronicles 7:14). Do we believe this? If we do, we should pray "Your kingdom come" every day.

As a D-Group leader, one thing you must lead your group to do every time you meet is to pray for revival and spiritual awakening in our land. As you take prayer requests, remind your group of this request every week.

As a student at Southwestern Baptist Theological Seminary in Fort Worth, Texas, I had the privilege to study under Dr. Roy Fish. In a class on Spiritual Awakening, I recall Dr. Fish teaching that there is one thing that has preceded every great spiritual awakening throughout history. That one thing was a grassroots movement of common people confessing their sins and crying out to God for revival.

I long to see that movement happen again. I long to see people meeting in D-Groups all over the world, confessing their sins, crying out to God for revival, and praying the words of our Lord's model prayer, "Your kingdom come!"

Nurturing faith in the power of prayer will always be a work in progress. Jesus frequently had to correct His disciples for "their littleness of faith." But as you lead your group to pray, your faith will grow. You will see answers, even when you may not expect them.

Over the years, I've had the privilege to pray with many men in my D-Groups and to rejoice over remarkable answers to prayer. I rejoice when I think about Terry and how God brought back his prodigal son. I rejoice when I think about Chris and how God restored his relationship with his brother. I rejoice when I think about Justin and how God provided for him and his wife to go on their first mission trip. And then, there is Danny.

Danny is my special brother in Christ. He came into my life a few years ago after his mother died. Danny took it hard. After the funeral, he came to my office for a visit. We discussed the emptiness that was in his life and how only Christ could fill that void.

There was one problem. Danny had been a practicing homosexual for many years. He felt he couldn't come to Christ. I explained to Danny about our sinful nature and how we are all born with certain issues. I explained that he was not responsible for what he was tempted to do but only for what he chose to do. This seemed to set Danny free. He surrendered his feelings to God while choosing to repent, place his trust in Christ, and walk in sexual purity.

His countenance changed immediately. He was a new man. He started meeting with my D-Group on Friday mornings at a local restaurant. I encouraged Danny to share his testimony with the men in our group when he felt he was ready. It took time for him to feel that he could trust the group with his story. After eight months, there was a morning when we were discussing where we would be if it were not for the grace of God. Danny's hands began to shake. and I knew what was coming. I silently prayed for him as he shared his story, and then we had a God moment. The men in our group got up, gathered around Danny, and began praying for him. I'm not sure what others in the restaurant were thinking, but I thought it was beautiful. Danny was greatly encouraged by this.

Over the years, there have been few people I have prayed for more than Danny. Not only have I prayed for his continued spiritual growth but also his physical health. As a severe diabetic who is HIV positive, Danny lost both legs up to his knees and several of his fingers. We often teased him that God was taking him to heaven one piece at a time. He also lost the function of his kidneys. He went to dialysis three times a week and knocked on death's door more than once. I have known few people as resilient as Danny.

After his third year of walking through the Bible with me in our D-Group, Danny asked if I thought he was ready to lead a group. With great joy in my heart, I told him he was. As a new D-Group leader, he began meeting with his first group at another local restaurant. After a few weeks, he called me and said, "Pastor Bill, you are not going to believe what happened!" A worker at the restaurant approached their table and asked for prayer over a struggle she was going through. Danny said, "We prayed for her, and I got to lead her to Christ." It was the first person he had ever led to Christ.

When I think about the remarkable transformation that took place in Danny's life, I realize once again the power of discipleship. He often told others that he wouldn't be where he was apart from the love and accountability of his D-Group.

Later, Danny started another D-Group with those who were in dialysis with him. He took them *D-Life Journals* and began discipling them. He recently led two other men to Christ who struggled with sexual identity issues and began discipling them.

I love Danny. He could have given a million reasons why he couldn't lead a D-Group, but he didn't make excuses. He made disciples and made a difference.

For some reason, Danny liked to talk to me about doing his funeral. I would tell him to stop and remind him that God wasn't through with him yet. It was amazing how God continued to preserve him. Unfortunately, I recently did conduct Danny's funeral after he lost a brief battle with COVID-19. I can only imagine the rewards that awaited him. He had a lot to overcome in his life, but now, he has two new legs, two new kidneys, and maybe even some hair for that bald head of his. To go with it, I am certain there are several stars in his crown.

## 🔍 Discussion Questions for a Small Group Study

1.  Why do you think the great power of fervent prayer is often neglected? How is your prayer life? Can you share a testimony about a recent answer to prayer? What is the best way for you to learn to pray and why?

2.  Why should you never meet with your D-Group and not pray? How can a simple thing like sharing weekly prayer requests turn into a breakthrough moment in your group? Why should you assign different people to lead in prayer each week? How should you handle it when someone is not comfortable with praying out loud?

3.  Read Matthew 6:9-13. In what ways is the Lord's Prayer a model for how you should pray? What is the ACTS acrostic and how can it help you remember the elements of a mature prayer? Why should mature believers pray mature prayers when praying with their group?

4.  What is the first actual request in the Lord's Prayer? In what ways is this petition a request for revival in our

land? Read 2 Chronicles 7:14. What great promise to claim is given in this verse? Why must you lead your D-Group to pray for revival and spiritual awakening in our land every time you meet?

5. In what ways is prayer like the "secret weapon" of the kingdom of God? Why is it important to pray intercessory prayers on behalf of others? Why is it important to humble yourself and share with others how they can pray for you? What is one thing for which you need prayer today?

**Closing Prayer:** Heavenly Father, thank You for the secret weapon of prayer. Forgive us when we show weak faith and pray shallow prayers. Boldly, we pray for Your kingdom to come and for Your will to be done on earth as in heaven.

# CHAPTER 8

# Outside The Walls

## The Ministry of D-Life

*He called the twelve and began to send them out two by two, and gave them authority over the unclean spirits. . . . So they went out and proclaimed that people should repent. And they cast out many demons and anointed with oil many who were sick and healed them.*
—Mark 6:7, 12–13

Justin is a D-Group leader. During his group's prayer time, he requested prayer for a local fire station that had recently lost a fireman to a brain aneurysm. The other firemen at the station were having a difficult time with the loss. The group began planning a ministry project for the men at the station. They coordinated the project with the fire chief and went to the station to grill steaks. Justin's D-Group prepared a full steak dinner for the firemen, prayed with them, and left each of them with a free New Testament that highlighted the message of the gospel.

Have you ever wondered why most ministry takes place inside the walls of the church? You don't see this with Jesus.

Almost all of the personal ministry of Jesus took place outside the walls of the temple or synagogue.

As believers who make up the church, the Bible says, "You are the body of Christ" (1 Corinthians 12:27). We are His hands and feet, but we often tie up His hands with matters inside the church. We fail to make a difference in the world when we keep His hands and feet inside the walls of the church.

Jesus said that we are "salt of the earth." But what good is salt if it remains in the shaker? He said, "It is no longer good for anything except to be thrown out and trampled under people's feet" (Matthew 5:13).

That's exactly what many do with the church. They throw it out as something irrelevant to their lives. The church has a perception problem that can only be changed by showing the world the love of Christ in practical ways. As a D-Group leader, you can influence this change by leading your group to do the work of ministry and evangelism outside the walls of the church.

Earlier, we saw that Jesus launched an unstoppable movement of common people who were big on social justice and sharing the good news of Christ. With no big buildings or budgets, the early disciples multiplied greatly and spread Jesus' fame across the earth. In contrast, we often spend more energy on church building projects and budget planning than we do spreading His fame. This must change, but the question is how?

Remember that everything rises or falls on disciple-making. In the New Testament, we see Jesus leading His disciples outside the walls of the synagogue to proclaim the message of the kingdom. His disciples watched as He touched the leper, healed the sick, fed the hungry, and showed compassion for the sinner. Then He "began to send them out two by two" to do the same (Mark 6:7). It was their turn. The Bible simply says, "So they went" (Mark 6:12).

In Jesus' D-Group, doing ministry outside the walls of the synagogue was not an option. It shouldn't be for us either; it's our turn. This is an important part of leading a D-Group.

You deceive yourself if you think you can disciple others solely from a classroom. Disciple-making requires on-the-job training. Would you fly on a plane with a pilot whose only training was in a classroom? Of course not. Pilots need real experience and so do disciples. Disciple-making requires a lab, and the world is our lab.

## Lead Your Group to Plan Meaningful Ministry Projects

In your D-Group, take time to plan for meaningful ministry. Don't just throw together some meaningless service project so you can check off the ministry box. There are real issues out there—victims of sex trafficking, refugees in crisis, latchkey children, hungry people, and many who are homeless.

It will be okay with Jesus if you skip a few Bible studies so that you can walk the love of Jesus into a world filled with hurt. How can you be the hands and feet of Jesus where His presence is needed most? Whiteboard this question with your group. Pray for the Holy Spirit to direct your path. Plan for meaningful ministry projects where you can bring light into darkness and hope to those who are hurting.

Such incarnational ministry is best fleshed out in a D-Group. Real people who rub shoulders daily with other real people know better than the church staff where the real needs are. "Serve Days" planned by ministry professionals are great for wearing a t-shirt, getting our hands dirty for Jesus, and doing some hard work for the kingdom. There is certainly nothing wrong with that. However, it is so much more impactful when it's organic. When an ordinary person crosses paths with someone who has desperate eyes, the need becomes real. Meaningful ministry happens when a disciple says, "I know where a real need is. I saw it with my own eyes." This is when a group takes ownership of the ministry that needs to be done.

I'm sure you have heard of the 80/20 principle. It's a principle that says 80 percent of the work in a church is carried out by only 20 percent of the people. This is a real concern for some people in the church today. But what is especially concerning is that the vast majority of the work done by the 20 percent takes place within the walls of the church. It makes you wonder if any percent of the work of ministry takes place outside the church

Think about Jesus and His disciples. What percentage of the twelve disciples did the work of ministry? All twelve—100 percent. Even Judas did, though he complained about it. Almost everything they did was outside-the-walls ministry.

How did this happen? It was because this is what Jesus had discipled them to do. In the church today, we could abolish the 80/20 principle if we could simply get the 20 percent to disciple the 80 percent to do the work of ministry. What's more, we could shift the focus of our ministry outside the walls of the church.

One September, my D-Group was brainstorming ministry project ideas. One of our guys reminded us of a lady in our church who was the director of an inner-city daycare. Since our group met at 6:00 a.m. anyway, he suggested that we set up tables with donuts, juice, and free evangelism Bibles to give to each family. Our group thought this was a good idea.

We secured the approval of the director and made plans for the project. At the time, I had eight men in my group as we prepared to multiply. How many of those men do you think showed up at 6:00 a.m. to walk the love of Christ over to an inner-city daycare? You guessed it, all eight. Why? Because that was how they were discipled. That's the power of disciple-making.

## Lead Your Group to Go Out and Do Meaningful Ministry Projects

After your group makes plans for a meaningful ministry, then go out and do it. Sharing in ministry together as a D-Group is both fun and fruitful. It builds a deeper community within your group.

Ministry projects may include things such as feeding the homeless, blessing someone with free lawn care, doing a project at a local school, building a wheelchair ramp, adopting a family for Christmas, prayer walk evangelism, offering assistance to other social ministries in your area, and many other creative ideas. The opportunities are endless. D-Groups can even make plans to go on a mission trip together.

A minimum goal for your group should be to do at least one meaningful ministry project every two months. This means that your D-Group will do six ministry projects a year. Again, it is important to keep your goals reasonable and attainable. If we truly desire to impact our world for Christ, this is a reasonable minimum goal.

Think about the significance of this on your church's ministry to your community. If your church started only four D-Groups, this would result in twenty-four ministry projects outside the walls of your church in one year. Simply multiplying to ten D-Groups would result in sixty ministry projects. What if someday you could train one hundred believers to lead D-Groups? This would result in six hundred ministry projects each year outside the walls of your church. Can you imagine how many lives would be touched? Think about how people's perception of your church would change. Some of the "nones" might even become some of your members.

The real beauty of this is that it is organic. The pastors of the church are not planning all the ministry projects. The people are. The pastors can focus their energy on equipping disciple-makers who do meaningful ministry through their D-Groups outside the walls of the church.

Why would any true lover of Jesus not want to see this happen in his or her church? Wouldn't this be more fruitful than continuing to grease the machinery of old barren programs? It has been said that the definition of insanity is doing the same thing over and over again and expecting a different result. Through building a disciple-making culture, the church could lead the cause of social justice in our land instead of lagging behind it. As a result, the fame of Jesus would begin to spread once again.

## Lead Your Group to Practice Lift-Up-Your-Eyes Evangelism

Meaningful ministry opens doors for gospel conversations. When unbelievers see the love of Jesus displayed in a practical way, they are more willing to listen to what we have to say.

As a D-Group leader, you want to lead your group to practice lift-up-your-eyes evangelism. Jesus instructed His disciples saying, "Look, I tell you, lift up your eyes, and see that the fields are white for harvest" (John 4:35). When your D-Group does a ministry project, lift up your eyes and see those who are around you. See those who are watching you and wondering why you are there. Look for an opportunity to share the gospel with them.

Kyle Martin, of Time to Revive (www.timetorevive.com), teaches a simple and effective approach to lift-up-your-eyes evangelism. God is using Kyle in incredible ways to bring people together from different faith experiences to share the gospel with their city. I've had the privilege to participate in a couple of Time to Revive events, and it is awesome to see hundreds of people coming together to go and share Christ with their neighbors.

If you were to go to a Time to Revive event, you would hear Kyle share four steps to effective servant evangelism. These are great principles to share with your D-Group as you prepare for a ministry project.

The first is to love. Every meaningful ministry project is motivated by love. We go out to show the love of Christ in a practical way. However, a big part of showing the love of Christ is to share the gospel of Christ. You want to engage in meaningful gospel conversations at every opportunity. Lift up your eyes and engage those around you in friendly conversation. Show your love and concern by asking, "Is there anything I can pray for you about?" This question will help you discern their feelings about God and may provide a good transition into a gospel conversation.

Next is to listen. Listen carefully to their answer to your question. Some may respond coldly and express no desire for prayer. However, others may respond warmly and share with you a prayer need.

Discern. Carefully discern how you should respond to each one. Be gentle with those who are cold and indifferent. Pray on the spot with those who share a prayer need. Pray specifically for their request.

Finally, respond. When you get a cold response, be courteous and respect others' space. With those who let you pray for them, proceed with a conversation about the gospel.

The *Revive New Testament* published by Life Bible Study (www.lifebiblestudy.org) is an excellent tool to use for sharing the gospel. Equip your D-Group with this Bible or another evangelism tool and teach them how to use it. As God opens hearts to the gospel, immediately invite them to be a part of your D-Group or help them connect with another group.

There are two very effective ways that we do evangelism through our D-Groups. If you think back to chapter 5, "Talking to Strangers," you were encouraged to invite an unbeliever to join your D-Group. This is someone you have built a relationship with and who is open to walking through the Bible with you. In disciple-making, you are not inviting people to your church, you are inviting them to come hang out with you. As an unbeliever begins to participate in a D-Group, he or she will likely be led to Christ organically through the witness of the group. At that point, you will lead them to connect with your church.

The second way you do evangelism is through meaningful ministry projects. As your D-Group goes out every other month to do a ministry project, they practice lift-up-your-eyes evangelism and engage others in gospel conversations. When they lead others to Christ, they will seek to connect them with their D-Group, and when possible, to your church.

In many churches today, intentional evangelism does not exist. No one is being discipled to share his or her faith. However, to be a true disciple-maker, you must unite evangelism and discipleship into one process. Think about it. You can do evangelism without being a disciple-maker, but you can't be a disciple-maker without doing evangelism.

If you are a fan of reality television, perhaps you've watched a series providing home improvements for less fortunate families. In the spring of 2018, a D-Group of women in our church brought a similar reality into the home of a young mother who was an immigrant living in Birmingham. With two young children and a baby on the way, the young mother obtained a restraining order against her abusive husband and moved into an unfurnished apartment. Her apartment was unfurnished, that is, until this group of ladies became aware of her need.

When they became aware of the young mother's situation, they were prepared for meaningful ministry. The women in the D-Group collected the furniture needed to completely furnish the apartment. They even provided a nursery for the baby and moved everything in while the mother was in the hospital. As she gave birth to her beautiful baby, she had no idea what she was about to come home to. It was truly an amazing home makeover. She brought her baby home to be welcomed by a loving group of women and a fully furnished apartment. This is a beautiful example of incarnational ministry and the power of disciple-making.

## 🔍 Discussion Questions for a Small Group Study

1.  For most churches, why do you think the majority of their ministries take place inside the walls of the church? How is this different from the example of Jesus and His disciples? Can you think of some specific instances of Jesus doing the work of ministry and evangelism outside the walls of a synagogue?

2.  Would you fly on a plane with a pilot whose only training was in a classroom? Why or why not? Why would someone think that he or she can effectively disciple others solely from a classroom? In true disciple-making, why must a D-Group leader provide on-the-job training in the areas of ministry and evangelism?

3.  Read Mark 6:7-12. In Jesus' D-Group, why was doing the work of ministry outside the walls of the synagogue not an option for His disciples? Why should it not be for us either? Can you think of some meaningful ministry projects that your D-Group could do outside the walls of your church?

4.  According to the author, how many ministry projects should every D-Group plan for and carry out each year? Do you agree that this is a reasonable and attainable goal? Why or why not? What impact do you think this would have on people's perception of your church?

5.  According to Kyle Martin, of Time to Revive, what are the four steps to effective servant evangelism? In true disciple-making, why must evangelism and discipleship be joined together into one process?

Why can you do evangelism without being a disciple-maker, but you can't be a disciple-maker without doing evangelism?

**Closing Prayer:** Heavenly Father, hurting people cross our paths every day. Help us to see them—to really see them. Prepare our hearts to show them Your love in practical ways and to share with them the gospel of Christ.

# CHAPTER 9
# Growth Without Gimmicks

## *The Multiplication of D-Life*

*You then, my child, be strengthened by the grace that is in Christ Jesus,
and what you have heard from me in the presence of many witnesses
entrust to faithful men, who will be able to teach others also.*
—2 Timothy 2:1–2

In November of 2017, Rondie and I traveled to Greensboro, North Carolina, to lead a D-Life Boot Camp at Lawndale Baptist Church. Associate Pastor Barry Owen invited us to come and train leaders in his men's ministry for a lifestyle of disciple-making. Compared to other training events, this was one of the smaller ones we have led, with only twelve men participating in the training. However, God was getting ready to do some big things.

Out of the twelve men who went through the training, eight started leading D-Groups in January of 2018. What began to happen in those eight groups became the talk of the church and conversations were taking place about starting groups for women and students. Barry planned another training event in

March and new D-Groups were started for college students, young adults, and women. Groups started multiplying throughout the community. In just two years, what started with eight men had multiplied to fifty D-Groups reaching over 250 people, many who were not members of the church.

Barry is leading his church to build a disciple-making culture. He and his wife, Diane, have become our great friends, and we love to hear from them about the exciting things God is doing in their church as they continue to multiply new discipleship groups.

Barry said, "God is multiplying this ministry in ways I can't keep up." He shared about an eighty-four-year-old man in their church who had been in a group for eight months. He wanted to reach men in his subdivision, so he left this group to start his own. None of the men in his subdivision attended his church, but he was concerned about the eternal destination of his neighbors. He started a new D-Group in his subdivision and had four to six men who began to show up every week. Barry said, "That's why you do D-Life."

Barry gets it. It's all about multiplication. This is why you lead a D-Group. Your goal is not to meet with your group until Jesus comes back. Your goal is to multiply. You want to make disciples who make disciples. This is growth without gimmicks. This is God's plan for how His kingdom is to advance on earth.

Many people today fail to grasp the significance of multiplication in discipleship. Because of this, the kingdom principle of multiplying disciples is often ignored. However, if you want to see revitalization in your church, multiplication is a must. Apart from multiplication, there is no real discipleship.

When Jesus invited twelve men to be in His discipleship group, He knew that He would not be with them forever. His goal was not to remain with them but to send them out. As disciples, these men were not the sharpest knives in the drawer. They were slow to learn, and their faith was small. However, Jesus' patience and perseverance with them paid off. In just three short years, He had prepared them for the greater work and multiplied them out to make new disciples.

Later in the Bible, we are introduced to a man named Paul. He was not one of the original disciples. When we first meet him, he is not a disciple at all. He was a skeptic who did not believe in Jesus and who persecuted those who did. Through a supernatural encounter with Jesus on a desert road, his life was radically changed. Paul the skeptic not only became a disciple of Jesus, but he went on to become one of the greatest disciple-makers who ever lived.

As a man on a mission, Paul's whole life was committed to making and multiplying disciples. He took groups of disciples with him on his missionary journeys and left behind disciple-making leaders in every city where he stopped. The impact of Paul's life cannot be measured because of his relentless commitment to the greater work.

Someone very special to Paul was a young disciple named Timothy. As he approached the end of his life on earth, Paul wrote a letter to his young disciple giving Timothy his own version of the Great Commission. With tenderness and strength, Paul said, "You then, my child, be strengthened by the grace that is in Christ Jesus, and what you have heard from me in the presence of many witnesses entrust to faithful men, who will be able to teach others also" (2 Timothy 2:1-2).

This is one of the clearest descriptions of genuine discipleship in the entire Bible. There is no way it can be misunderstood that multiplication is an essential quality of discipleship. According to Paul, multiplication is a disciple maker's mandate. As a D-Group leader, you must lead your group to multiply.

## The Multiplication of Disciples Is Empowered

Knowing that the time for his departure was at hand, Paul realized that Timothy would need God's strength to carry on the greater work he had trained him to do. With the love of a father, he encouraged Timothy to "be strengthened by the grace that is in Christ Jesus" (2 Timothy 2:1). The word translated "strengthened" is the Greek word *endunamoó*. From the root of this word, we get the word *dynamite*. Here, Paul was reminding Timothy that God's grace would be with him to empower him for making disciples.

The same is true for you. As you lead your D-Group, God will be with you. The Spirit of the greatest disciple-maker who ever lived dwells in you. He is the Spirit that raised Jesus from the dead. He will continually empower you with great strength and explosive power to make disciples who make disciples.

## The Multiplication of Disciples Is Explained

So, what exactly does it mean to be a disciple-maker? What specifically has God empowered you to do? Nowhere in the New Testament is the process of disciple-making more clearly laid out as Paul explains it here.

Paul said, "What you have heard from me in the presence of many witnesses entrust to faithful men, who will be able to teach others also" (2 Timothy 2:2). In this one sentence, we see four generations of discipleship: (1) Paul, (2) Timothy, (3) faithful men, and (4) others also. Paul had discipled Timothy.

Now it was Timothy's turn to disciple some faithful men. In turn, these faithful men were to disciple others also.

This is how God's kingdom is intended to grow. This is growth without gimmicks. The great expansion of the early church did not happen by addition. It was the result of the explosive process of multiplication. Concerning the early church, the Bible says, "And the word of God continued to increase, and the number of the disciples multiplied greatly" (Acts 6:7).

When you step up to lead a D-Group, you are on the front lines of the advancement of God's kingdom on earth. It's not the preacher in the pulpit but the disciple-maker in the trenches who determines if the kingdom grows. It is important you do your job. You are empowered for this. Don't be duped by the misleading allure of addition. Simply put, your job is not to grow a bigger group but to multiply new groups. It's only through the multiplication of disciples that you will witness the result of exponential kingdom growth.

As a true disciple-maker, you must make multiplication your primary goal. Intentionally and methodically, strive to send out at least one new disciple-maker every year to lead a new D-Group. You may not always achieve this goal, but you should make it your aim. This is a reasonable and worthy objective.

According to the Bible, the Father is glorified when "you bear much fruit" (John 15:8). Perhaps, you do not realize the greatness of your fruit-bearing potential. When you live a lifestyle of disciple-making, you possess the unlimited potential to bear much fruit and to bring great glory to the Father.

Consider the possibilities. What if you simply discipled three people every year—just three? Then, what if you sent out one of them each year to do the same? If this became your lifestyle for the next twenty to thirty years, the fruit of your life would be immeasurable.

Let's take a deeper look. As a D-Group leader, here is your goal:

- You simply disciple at least three people every year.
- You send out one disciple each year to do the same.

As you make disciples who make disciples, the unlimited nature of your fruit-bearing potential is seen in the chart below.

---

## THE POWER OF THE GREATER WORK

**Y1** = 1 D-Group / 3 People
**Y2** = 2 D-Groups / 6 People
**Y3** = 4 D-Groups / 12 People
**Y4** = 8 D-Groups / 24 People
**Y5 = 16 D-Groups / 48 People**

**Y6** = 32 D-Groups / 96 People
**Y7** = 64 D-Groups /192 People
**Y8** = 128 D-Groups / 384 People
**Y9** = 256 D-Groups / 768 People
**Y10 = 512 D-Groups / 1,536 People**

**Y11** = 1,024 D-Groups / 3,072 People
**Y12** = 2,048 D-Groups / 6,144 People
**Y13** = 4,096 D-Groups / 12,288 People
**Y14** = 8,192 D-Groups / 24,576 People
**Y15 = 16,384 D-Groups / 49,152 People**

**Y16** = 32,768 D-Groups / 98,304 People
**Y17** = 65,536 D-Groups / 196,608 People
**Y18** = 131,072 D-Groups / 393,216 People
**Y19** = 262,144 D-Groups / 786,432 People
**Y20 = 524,288 D-Groups / 1,572,864 People**

**Y21** = 1,048,576 D-Groups / 3,145,728 People
**Y22** = 2,097,152 D-Groups / 6,291,456 People
**Y23** = 4,194,304 D-Groups / 12,582,912 People
**Y24** = 8,388,608 D-Groups / 25,165,824 People
**Y25 = 16,777,216 D-Groups / 50,331,648 People**

**Y26** = 33,554,432 D-Groups / 100,663,296 People
**Y27** = 67,108,864 D-Groups / 201,326,592 People
**Y28** = 134,217,728 D-Groups / 402,653,184 People
**Y29** = 268,435,356 D-Groups / 805,306,368 People
**Y30 = 536,870,912 D-Groups / Over 1.5 Billion People**

---

Wow! This is your fruit-bearing potential for the Father. In just ten years, over five hundred discipleship groups and more than fifteen hundred disciples could trace their roots back to you. In twenty years, over five hundred thousand discipleship groups and a million and a half people would be discipled because of you. In thirty years—well, we won't even go there—but as my friend, Barry said, "This is why you do D-Life."

I know what you are thinking. Like the twelve disciples, you may not consider yourself the sharpest knife in the drawer. You're thinking that such a disciple-making movement could never happen because of you. But why not you? Don't you think the early disciples must have thought the same?

Nevertheless, it all begins with just three and one—discipling three people a year and multiplying one out to do the same. If you could have the faith to do just this, you have the potential to reach thousands of people for Christ. That's a lot of fruit. Why would you not want to do the greater work?

Exponential kingdom growth is the ultimate result of multiplying disciples. When I think about the raw reality of this, my heart weeps over the failure of the church to do our job. Disciple-making is our job! Jesus taught it, modeled it, and commanded it. Paul taught it, modeled it, and commanded it. We have no excuse.

In thirty-three years, just one person has the potential to reach the entire globe for Christ. But wait, what if there were more than one person? A global grassroots disciple-making movement would mean that the world is still within our reach.

I believe this movement has already begun. There is an army rising up. It's an army of people from all nations, tribes, and languages. It's a blue-collar army of genuine disciple-makers who believe in the power of the greater work.

## The Multiplication of Disciples Is Expected

Before his departure, Paul reminded Timothy that it was his turn. He clearly laid out what was expected of him as a follower of Christ. This same call is expected of us.

**To begin, you must have the dedication of a soldier.**
Paul said, "Share in suffering as a good soldier of Christ
Jesus. No soldier gets entangled in civilian pursuits, since his
aim is to please the one who enlisted him" (2 Timothy 2:3-
4). In a day when spiritual narcissism has infested the church,
suffering as a good soldier is not a trendy message. It doesn't
fit the narrative nor does it draw the crowd. It may send some
scurrying to the church down the road. Many have no desire
to be inconvenienced for the gospel of the kingdom. The
expectation to make disciples for Christ is not on the list of
many church shoppers. However, Paul didn't have time to
mince words and neither do we. How inconvenienced are you
willing to be to make disciples?

"Civilian pursuits" have caused many believers to go
AWOL from the Great Commission. They are absent without
leave from the greater work. "I don't have the time," they say,
"I'm discipling my family." Absolutely. We must disciple our
families, but we don't have to go anywhere to do that. The
Great Commission of our Lord calls for us to go and make
disciples of all nations. You are at your best in discipling your
family when you obey God's call to go and make disciples.
Many say they have no time to make disciples; however, they
have ample time for ball tournaments and dance competitions
on the Lord's Day. Ouch, that stings. It's not that we shouldn't
enjoy sports or dance competitions with our families, but why
not use the connections you make through these events to start
a discipleship group?

Paul reminded Timothy that good soldiers and disciple-
makers must not get entangled in civilian pursuits. If you aim
to please the One who enlisted you, you will lay aside all civilian
pursuits that keep you from the greater work.

**Next, you must have the discipline of an athlete.** Paul said, "An athlete is not crowned unless he competes according to the rules" (2 Timothy 2:5). Being a disciple-maker will require some spiritual discipline. You must have the discipline to fish for some people and to keep on fishing until you catch a few to join with you in a D-Group. You must have the discipline to read your Bible daily and keep notes on your application points. There must be the discipline to lead your group to plan and carry out meaningful ministry projects outside the walls of the church. Above all, you must have the discipline to work diligently to multiply out new leaders.

Yes, a measure of spiritual discipline is required to lead a D-Group, but you can do this. Paul encouraged Timothy to run well and to compete for the crown according to the rules. To compete according to the rules means to follow the process. Likewise, I encourage you to follow the simple process for disciple-making that Jesus modeled for you. It's a process that cannot fail. If you follow it, you will do well and be certain to receive a heavenly crown.

**Finally, you must have the diligence of a farmer.** Paul said, "It is the hard-working farmer who ought to have the first share of the crops. Think over what I say, for the Lord will give you understanding in everything" (2 Timothy 2:6-7). A "hard-working farmer" is a great analogy for disciple-making. Farmers work hard to prepare the soil and to plant the seed. It requires patience and diligence. However, every farmer knows that he has no control over the weather. Ultimately, the growth of the crop comes from the Lord.

For a hard-working farmer, the greatest reward is the harvest. Likewise, the greatest reward in disciple-making is multiplication. As a D-Group leader, you must diligently plant the seed of God's Word into the lives of those you disciple, and you must patiently prepare them for leadership. There is no greater joy than making disciples who make disciples.

Now come in close, this is important. A wise farmer knows when the crop is ready for harvest. He also knows when it is not ready and needs more time to grow. Likewise, a wise D-Group leader knows when a disciple is ready to lead. He also knows when one is not ready and needs more time to grow.

The worst thing you can do is to multiply out someone to lead a new D-Group who is not ready to lead. How will you know? The Lord will give you discernment. Some may not be ready to lead until they have walked through the Bible with you for three or four years. Those who lack discipline in their daily Bible reading, have weak theology, or continue to struggle with moral issues are not ready to lead. Be patient with them and continue to disciple them toward spiritual maturity. It will be very rewarding to watch them eventually grow into the leader that God means for them to be. Think about how patient and persistent Jesus was with His disciples, especially Peter. What joy it must have brought Jesus to see Peter eventually mature into the rock-solid leader that He trained him to be.

The second worst thing you can do is to not multiply out someone to lead a new D-Group who is ready to lead. Mature believers that you have recruited to help with the group may be ready to lead within a year or less. Resist the temptation to keep them in your group because of your fellowship and friendship with them. They will continue to be your friend even if they multiply out to lead a new group. Remember that the advancement of God's kingdom is more important than the enjoyment of your fellowship. There will always be new friends to bring into the fellowship of your D-Group.

## The Multiplication of Disciples Is Exciting

As a D-Group leader, you will discover that disciple-making is one of the most fulfilling and rewarding things you will ever do. It's exciting to lead a D-Group. It truly is the greater work. There is great peace that comes with living out your supreme purpose in life. Your life will bear much fruit for the Father and bring Him glory.

As Paul's life came to a close, he said to Timothy, "the time of my departure has come. I have fought the good fight, I have finished the race, I have kept the faith. Henceforth there is laid up for me the crown of righteousness, which the Lord, the righteous judge, will award to me on that day, and not only to me but also to all who have loved his appearing" (2 Timothy 4:6–8). These are not the sad last words of a dying man. These are words of triumph. Paul understood his purpose in life and had run the race well. He knew that the crown of righteousness would soon be his reward. It's almost as if there was a hint of excitement about the time of his departure.

As a lead pastor, there will come a time when I will need to step down from my role and let a younger man of God take my place. However, by the grace of God, I will never step down from being a disciple-maker. As long as I have breath, I will be leading a D-Group and making disciples who make disciples. It's my supreme purpose and the greater work that God has called me to do. Like Paul, I want to run the race well to the finish line.

When the time for my departure has come, I pray that I can say with Paul that I have fought the good fight, I have finished the race, and I have kept the faith. I pray that I will leave behind the legacy of a long line of disciples who are making disciples.

Finally, I pray that my life will have been abundantly fruitful for the glory of my Father. With all my heart, I pray the same for you.

## 🔍 Discussion Questions for a Small Group Study

1. Why do you think many people fail to grasp the significance of multiplication in discipleship? To see revitalization in your church, why is the multiplication of disciples a must? How did both Jesus and Paul model a multiplying process of disciple-making?
2. Read 2 Timothy 2:1-2. What four generations of discipleship can you identify in this passage? When you make disciples who make disciples, how does this result in growth without gimmicks? For the kingdom of God to grow on earth, why is the disciple-maker in the trenches more important than the preacher in the pulpit?
3. If you simply disciple at least three people every year and send out one each year to do the same, what is your fruit-bearing potential in ten years? What is it in twenty years? What about thirty years? With this in mind, why would you not want to lead a D-Group?
4. Read 2 Timothy 2:3-7. In what ways must a disciple-maker have the dedication of a soldier? In what ways must one have the discipline of an athlete? In what ways must one have the diligence of a farmer? How inconvenienced are you willing to be to make disciples who make disciples?
5. According to the author, what is the greatest reward of disciple-making? How can you know when someone is not ready to lead a new D-Group and how should

you respond? When someone is ready to lead, why is the advancement of God's kingdom more important than the enjoyment of your fellowship?

**Closing Prayer:** Father, forgive us for our feeble attempts to expand your kingdom by addition. Thank you for the example of Jesus, who modeled a multiplying process of discipleship. Grant that our lives may bear much fruit for you as we commit ourselves to the greater work of making disciples who make disciples.

# CHAPTER 10

# Do Your Job

## The Accountability of D-Life

*"Simon, Simon, behold, Satan demanded to have you, that he might sift you like wheat, but I have prayed for you that your faith may not fail. And when you have turned again, strengthen your brothers." Peter said to him, "Lord, I am ready to go with you both to prison and to death." Jesus said, "I tell you, Peter, the rooster will not crow this day, until you deny three times that you know me."*
—Luke 22:31–34

As the father of three boys, I've spent a lot of time at the ballpark. All of my sons were good athletes and my middle son, Jake, received a scholarship to play football as a running back for the Samford University Bulldogs in Homewood, Alabama. Over the years, I've sat through hundreds of ball practices from little league through college. The sounds and smells of football practice are etched in my memory. At every phase of the sport, I could always hear a coach yelling across a football field at the top of his lungs, "Just do your job! Don't worry about anyone else. Just do your job!"

As believers in Christ, it's time for us to do our job. Our job is the Great Commission. The Lord Jesus Christ has given us a crystal-clear mandate to make disciples who make disciples. This is our greater work, and a lost world is desperate for us to do our job.

In this chapter, we come to the last of the six practices of D-Life, which are: (1) fellowship, (2) teaching, (3) prayer, (4) ministry, (5) multiplication, and (6) accountability. In many ways, accountability is the glue that holds it all together. It's the engine that drives the entire disciple-making process. Without accountability, it can all fall apart.

As a D-Group leader, you must provide loving, spiritual accountability for your group. This is crucial to your success as a leader. Without personal accountability, the other five practices of disciple-making are destined to fail.

Jesus provides a great example of spiritual accountability. Toward the end of His ministry, He warned Simon Peter that Satan had requested to "sift him like wheat" (Luke 22:31). He told Peter that He was praying for him and, when he turned back again, he should strengthen his brothers. Being the hardhead that he was, Peter took offense. He told Jesus he was ready to go the distance with Him, even to death. Yet Jesus, knowing His friend, laid the truth at his feet by telling Peter he'd deny him not once but three times before morning.

We know where this is going. Just as Christ said, Peter blatantly denied Jesus to those around him. On his third denial, throwing in a few choice words, he said, "I don't know what you are talking about."

Immediately, while Peter was still speaking, the rooster crowed, "Cock-a-doodle-do!" Peter was a broken man. The only thing he knew to do was to go back to his old way of life.

He felt like an utter failure and a disappointment as a disciple. He had denied his teacher and Lord. He had flunked out of Discipleship Class 101. Three years earlier, he had dropped his fishing net and left everything to follow after Jesus. Now, he picked his net back up and returned to the one thing he knew how to do. It was the one thing he felt he was good at. He went back to being a fisherman. He went back to being Simon, which was his name before Jesus changed it to Peter—the Rock. He sure didn't feel like a rock at this point in his life.

If it were not for the loving accountability of Jesus, Simon might not have ever returned to being Peter again. He may have spent the rest of his life living with guilt and regret, thinking about what might have been.

But let's leave this story here for now. We will return later to examine the beautiful way that Jesus responded to Peter. First, I want us to consider the vital role that accountability plays in the disciple-making process.

## Lives Are Changed Through Spiritual Accountability

As a D-Group leader, you must hold your group accountable in three important areas of spiritual development. It is vital for you to do your job in this area. It has often been said that people don't do what they are supposed to do, they do what they are held accountable to do. That is why loving spiritual accountability is a very important part of the disciple-making process.

**First, there must be accountability to the Word of God.** Holding your group accountable for their daily Bible reading will have a great impact on their lives. People who have never read the Bible with consistency will begin to read it daily. This alone is transformational.

Remember, it is very important to ask your group the two weekly accountability questions at every meeting: (1) Did everyone read your daily Bible reading assignments? (2) What are some of the application points that you found? Be sure to look each one in the eyes and have them answer these two questions.

In addition, D-Group leaders should email and text those in their group regularly to encourage them in their commitment to reading the Bible. Emails and text messages are quick and easy tools to use for encouragement and accountability.

**Next, there must be accountability to our walk with God.** As you lead your group to discuss the great stories of the Bible, be sure to ask questions that hold your group accountable to the main points of the story. Don't be afraid to ask questions related to the Bible text that are more personal. It is important in discipleship for those in your group to be real with one another.

When someone in your group is struggling in a certain area of his or her spiritual life, it is important to provide personal accountability. Spiritual strongholds related to alcohol, drugs, pornography, sexual identity issues, and others can be overcome through the loving accountability of a D-Group.

**Finally, there must be accountability to our work and witness for God**. As a D-Group leader, the goal for your group is to work together on at least one ministry and evangelism project every two months. Six times each year you are to hold one another accountable to go outside the walls of the church to show the love of Christ in practical ways and to share the gospel of Christ.

Ministry and evangelism are vital parts of the disciple-making process. You must lead your group to do missional ministry. This will not happen by accident. You must hold your group accountable to be faithful servants and witnesses for Christ.

## Leaders Are Called Through Spiritual Accountability

Let's return to our story about Simon Peter. After denying Jesus three times, Peter felt like a failure. He was ready to quit and throw in the towel as a disciple of Christ. He planned to return to his former trade as a fisherman, but Jesus had another plan. Jesus went to Peter to restore him and to hold him accountable for his commitment as a disciple.

One night, while Peter was fishing with his friends, the risen Jesus went to them and stood on the shore of the sea. Unrecognized at first, He asked the men if they had caught any fish. When they answered no, He instructed them to cast the net on the right side of the boat.

For Peter, this was déjà vu. Remember, this had happened earlier in Peter's walk as a disciple and it totally wrecked him. He and his companions hauled in such a great catch of fish that the Bible said, "their nets were breaking" (Luke 5:6). It was then that Peter fell down on his knees and confessed his sins to Jesus as his Lord (Luke 5:8). I believe this was the moment when he experienced true salvation. Lovingly, Jesus was taking a broken and humbled Peter back to that moment when he first believed.

Three years had passed since Peter brought in his first great catch of fish. Now, Jesus asked Peter once again to let down his nets for a catch. Unlike before, there was no hesitation. As soon as the net hit the water, it filled up with large fish, 153 of them to be exact. Although there were so many, this time the Bible says that "the net was not torn" (John 21:11).

There is a big point in this tiny detail. It was a picture of Peter's growth as a disciple. Peter didn't know it yet, but the broken net was now mended. He was finally ready to be a fisher of men, fully equipped for the greater work that Jesus had called him to do.

When Peter saw the great catch of fish, he didn't wait on the boat to come to shore. He jumped out of the boat to swim to Jesus.

Jesus' model of loving accountability with Peter is an example to follow. Three times he had denied Jesus, and three times Jesus confronted him with his commitment as a disciple. He didn't say, "Peter, I told you so." He didn't condemn him for his failures. Instead, Jesus gave Peter three opportunities to tell Him that he loved Him and three reminders of his call as a disciple to "feed my sheep" (John 21:15–17).

Jesus was patient and loving with Peter, but He held him accountable for his commitment to the greater work. Despite his failures and shortcomings, Jesus reminded him that he was called to make disciples who make disciples. Lovingly, Jesus said to him, "Do your job." Through his brokenness and humility, Peter was finally ready to become a fisher of men.

This is true for every one of us. Regardless of our failures, insecurities, inadequacies, and shortcomings, we are called to be disciple-makers. We are called to do our job.

## Let Us Commit Our Lives to the Greater Work

A very humble Peter was reconciled to Jesus. The rest of the story is history. He became one of the greatest disciple-makers the world has ever known. He became the rock that Jesus always knew he could be. He preached the first sermon of the New Testament church and launched a disciple-making movement that turned the world upside down.

Humble people make great disciple-makers. They are willing to listen and learn. How about you? At some point, you must humble yourself and take a long, hard look in the mirror. You must ask yourself some tough questions. Am I a true disciple-maker? Am I living in obedience to the Great Commission? Am I doing the greater work of making disciples who make disciples?

Jesus said, "Truly, truly, I say to you, whoever believes in me will also do the works that I do; and greater works than these will he do, because I am going to the Father" (John 14:12). He didn't say you "might" do the works that He did. He said that you "will" do them. He didn't say you will make fewer disciples than Him. He said you will do "greater works" of disciple-making than Him. How is this possible?

According to Jesus, it's simple. It all begins with a small group of people who meet anytime and anywhere for intentional discipleship. This is how Jesus taught us to do it. To do the greater work involves either participating in a discipleship group or leading one. You should participate in a D-Group until you are ready to lead one. Then you should multiply out to begin a new one. This is how Jesus taught us to live a lifestyle of disciple-making.

Leading a D-Group is fun, fruitful, and fulfilling. It doesn't require great talent or ability, just availability, and devotion. Jesus had only three short years to disciple twelve men, but we have a lifetime to make disciples.

Therefore, you have a decision to make. Will you do your job? Take a moment to spend some time in prayer and let the Holy Spirit guide your heart. Then, I pray that you will commit your life to the greater work of making disciples who make disciples. This is life's ultimate commitment for a follower of Christ.

Remember, to lead a group effectively, D-Group leaders often need a good track to run on and a simple tool to keep them on track. We have you covered on this with D-Life Online or the *D-Life Journal*. For more information go to: www.livethedlife.com. To view samples of these materials, see appendixes 1 and 2.

## 🔍 Discussion Questions for a Small Group Study

1. In this chapter, we covered the last of the six practices of disciple-making. Briefly review what these six practices are. In what ways is accountability the glue that holds the entire process together? Without accountability, how can it all fall apart?

2. In what three important areas of spiritual development must a D-Group leader hold his or her group accountable? What two important questions must a leader ask every week to hold the group accountable to the reading of God's Word? How can emails and text messages be quick and easy tools to use for accountability?

3. As you lead your group to discuss the great stories of the Bible, how can you hold your group accountable for their personal walk with God? When someone in your group is struggling with a certain moral issue or spiritual stronghold, how can the loving accountability of a D-Group help this person to overcome it?

4. How can a leader hold one's group accountable to their work and witness for God? According to the author, how many ministry and evangelism projects should a D-Group work together on each year? Why is this great goal unlikely to happen by accident?

5. How is Jesus' model of loving accountability to Peter an example to follow? Do you think Simon Peter would have ever become the leader that God meant for him to be without personal accountability? Why or why not? Are you willing to do your job and to make a personal commitment to a lifestyle of disciple-making?

**Closing Prayer:** Heavenly Father, thank you for those in my life who have provided loving spiritual accountability. Help me to do the same for others as I commit to a lifestyle of disciple-making.

# PART 3
# DEVOTING TO THE GREATER WORK

# CHAPTER 11

# The Golden Calf

*And Moses said to Aaron, "What did this people do to you that you have brought such a great sin upon them?" And Aaron said, "Let not the anger of my lord burn hot. You know the people, that they are set on evil. For they said to me, 'Make us gods who shall go before us. As for this Moses, the man who brought us up out of the land of Egypt, we do not know what has become of him.' So I said to them, 'Let any who have gold take it off.' So they gave it to me, and I threw it into the fire, and out came this calf."*
—Exodus 32:21–24

Church revitalization has become a trendy topic at ministry conferences. There is a good reason for this. Most churches need revival and ministry leaders are eager to learn about this important issue. But how many times have you attended a session on the subject only to leave without a tangible plan for achieving it? Let's be honest. The best way to experience revitalization in your church is to build a disciple-making culture.

A great number of churches have an "Aaron's calf" approach to discipleship. Do you recall the story of Moses and Aaron in the wilderness of Sinai? After leading the Israelites out of Egypt, Moses left them in the wilderness to go up on Mount Sinai to meet with God. He left his brother Aaron in charge and was gone for a long time. When the people saw that Moses was delayed, they pressured Aaron to make them a god who would go before them. So, he asked the people to give him their rings of gold. After receiving the gold, he fashioned it with a graving tool to make a golden calf. The next day, the people rose early to offer sacrifices and dance in worship to the golden calf.

After receiving the Ten Commandments, Moses came down from the mountain. His anger burned hot when he saw the calf and the people dancing around it. When he confronted his brother about the golden calf, Aaron's explanation is both humorous and outrageous. Any five-year-old could come up with a better excuse. After explaining to Moses how he got the gold, he said, "I threw it into the fire and out came this calf" (Exodus 32:24). Really, Aaron? Is that the best you could do? This has to be the worst excuse of all time.

The problem is that church leaders often make a similar excuse. We ask our members to give us their valuable time. Then, we fire up our church programs and toss in the people. Our hopes are high that out will come a disciple-maker, but one seldom does. Really, pastors? Is this the best we can do?

Jesus did not teach us to have discipleship programs. He taught us how to make disciples who make disciples. The issue is that many of our church programs have become golden calves, and people often love the programs of the church more than they love the mission of the church. This is a problem. In fact, it is idolatry. It's time to repent and return to the greater work of our Great Commission.

The question is, how? Must we bury our church programs to revitalize the church? Maybe some, but certainly not all of them. One thing is essential. A tangible plan for church revitalization begins with building a disciple-making culture.

How can you build a true disciple-making culture in your church? How can you transition from merely having a discipleship program to making disciples who make disciples? Let's consider a five-step plan to build a disciple-making culture for church revitalization.

## Pray It Through

First and foremost, we must pray it through. We are not the first ministry leaders with a vision to revitalize and rebuild. Years ago, the word of the Lord came to Zerubbabel and said, "Not by might, nor by power, but by my Spirit, says the LORD of hosts" (Zechariah 4:6).

Church revitalization will never occur through human power and ingenuity. It will require a movement of the Holy Spirit. To lead the church in transition, we must pray it through. Pray with as many people as possible and as often as possible. Confess our sins to God and pray for revival in our church.

Times of change in a church will always bring challenges. Don't be surprised by this. At each step of the way, remember the word of the Lord to Zerubbabel and pray it through.

## Unite Your Leaders

The second step is to unite our leaders. This begins with the lead pastor. Building a disciple-making culture requires a disciple-making pastor. Without their bold and active leadership, it will be difficult to accomplish this goal. Lead pastors can guide from the first chair or the second chair, but they must not be passive. Strong leadership from lead pastors is essential.

It is also important to have a unified leadership team. Disunity will disrupt good plans. Work hard to bring everyone along. Include other ministers, deacons, and additional key leaders in the process. Meet regularly with the main influencers in your church to seek their wisdom and support. Communicate the vision with them and get them to join in praying it through.

Consider taking key leaders through a study of this book. This will help to keep everyone on the same page. As they work through the questions at the end of each chapter, they will join you in some great discussions and grow in understanding of what you, and they, seek to build. You cannot build something that cannot be seen. Likewise, the leaders must share a vision of a disciple-making culture before everyone can work together to build one.

## Develop a Process

The third step is essential. After uniting your leaders and praying it through, it is time to develop a disciple-making process. This is the missing link for most churches. One cannot build a disciple-making culture without a well-defined process to develop disciple-making people.

A disciple-making process is a clear and simple plan for making disciples who make disciples. It's not a program or curriculum, but it's a highly intentional process to equip and empower people for a lifestyle of disciple-making. Intentionality is the key word. Our great commission to make disciples is not something to leave to chance. It requires strategic intentionality.

When Jesus said, "Follow me, and I will make you fishers of men," He was both strategic and intentional (Matthew 4:19). He knew exactly what He wanted to make, and He knew how to make them. He was going to make disciples who make disciples.

Let's be honest. Few churches have any type of ministry that remotely resembles the relationship between Jesus and His disciples. As we have learned, Jesus taught us to make disciples in the relational environment of a small discipleship group. From His example, we know that a D-Group serves a three-fold purpose: (1) to grow in spiritual maturity, (2) to serve in missional ministry, and (3) to reproduce disciple-makers.

As close as possible, we want to develop a disciple-making process that resembles the one of Jesus and His disciples. There are a few good resources available for your church to look through. However, look for a true disciple-making process and not merely a small group curriculum. This process must include a clear path to equip your people for a lifestyle of disciple-making. Pray fervently for the Lord to lead you to the one that is right for you. I highly recommend D-Life for your consideration.

## Rethink the Model

The fourth step is to rethink your model for ministry. Once you develop a disciple-making process, define how it relates to other ministries in the church. You want your disciple-making process to be central to everything you do. However, you don't want it to create confusion in the congregation or a sense of competition within ministries. Strive for others to see your disciple-making process as something that complements your other ministries instead of something that competes with them.

One way to rethink your model for ministry is to consider the illustration of an atom. Around 400 BC, a very smart man named Democritus, a Greek philosopher, came up with the idea of the atom. He figured out that everything in the universe must be made up of tiny particles that are so small they cannot be cut. He called these particles "atoms," which comes from the Greek word *atomos*, meaning "indivisible" or "uncuttable." His remarkable theory remained a mostly philosophical topic until the development of chemistry in the 1600s.

Over the years, brilliant chemists and physicists discovered that atoms were real. They also learned that the enormous power of an atom is found in its nucleus. Revolving around the nucleus are different particles of the atom, which make each atom unique.

Likewise, most churches have a variety of programs that make them unique. They have great ministries related to worship, Bible study, Christian service, and missions. Though each of these ministries stands alone in importance, what they need is a clearly defined nucleus at the core of the church to provide energy and power for growth.

Lexico defines the "nucleus" as the central and most important part of an object, movement, or group, forming the basis for its activity and growth. Having a clear disciple-making process at the nucleus of your church will provide strategic intentionality for all of your other ministries. Everyone will know exactly what you are wanting to make and how you are planning to make it.

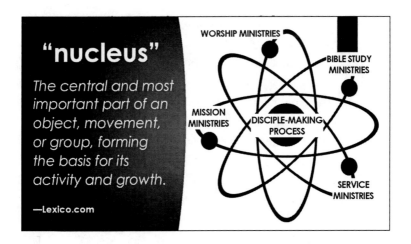

**"nucleus"**

The central and most important part of an object, movement, or group, forming the basis for its activity and growth.

—Lexico.com

WORSHIP MINISTRIES
BIBLE STUDY MINISTRIES
MISSION MINISTRIES
DISCIPLE-MAKING PROCESS
SERVICE MINISTRIES

Churches with an Aaron's calf approach to discipleship are like an atom with no nucleus. They hope to make disciples but are neither strategic nor intentional. They have discipleship programs but fail to produce disciple-makers. This is not what Jesus taught us to do. He did not call institutions to make disciples, but individuals. Likewise, the main purpose of the church is not merely to make disciples but to train up an army of disciple-makers to go do the greater work.

With a true disciple-making process at the nucleus of your church, you can train your people for a lifestyle of disciple-making. Individuals will begin to make and multiply disciples anytime and anywhere. As a result, you can ignite a disciple-making movement at the core of your ministries that will revitalize your church and provide great energy and power for growth.

In the 1930s, two German scientists, Otto Hahn and Fritz Strassmann, discovered that the "uncuttable" atom could be cut. Through a process of physics known as nuclear fission, they successfully split the nucleus of an atom, which resulted in the release of a great amount of energy. This release of energy is what makes nuclear fission useful today for making nuclear power plants or nuclear bombs.

Many years ago, a carpenter from Nazareth and twelve common men revealed a process of disciple-making that we could call "spiritual fission." They successfully split a D-Group, which resulted in the release of a great amount of energy, and "the number of the disciples multiplied greatly" (Acts 6:7). This release of energy is what makes spiritual fission useful today for building a disciple-making culture and reaching many people for Christ.

One more thing. What holds it all together? When you think about an atom, this was a question that confounded scientists for many years. The force that holds the particles of an atom together must be very strong. With a vivid display of imagination, physicists named this force "the strong force." Likewise, when you place disciple-making at the core of your church, something very strong will hold it together. That strong force is Jesus Christ. When you put disciple-making in the center, you are putting Jesus at the center of everything you do.

Rethinking your model for ministry is an important step to building a disciple-making culture for revitalization. Meet with your leaders and pray it through.

## Set Some Goals

The fifth and final step is to set goals. It's often said that if you aim for nothing, you'll hit it every time. Don't aim for nothing. Set some big goals. You now have a process in place to make them achievable, and you want to see the fruit of your labor. This is the fun part. Work with the leadership team to develop

SMART goals that are specific, measurable, achievable, realistic, and timely.

Your priority is to set disciple-making goals. This will give you the metrics you need to come back later and set goals for other ministries. So, where do we begin in setting our disciple-making goals? First, you must answer two big questions:

- How many D-Groups can you start with?
- At what rate can you expect them to multiply?

To answer the first question, you must train some leaders to start some D-Groups. Once you know how many D-Groups you can start with, then begin to set disciple-making goals. Start with only those you feel are fully equipped and devoted to lead a D-Group for multiple years.

To answer the second question, work with your leaders to determine the rate you can expect the groups to multiply each year. Your D-Group Multiplication Rate (DMR) is very important. Pray it through.

Answering these questions will likely lead to a crisis of belief. It will stretch your faith. However, with a true disciple-making process at the core of your church, you can experience the power of spiritual fission and multiply disciples at a rate unthought of before. Diligently seek God's leadership, remembering that "without faith it is impossible to please him" (Hebrews 11:6).

Once you know how many D-Groups you can start with and at what rate you can expect them to multiply, you are ready to set some exciting goals. Let's consider a couple of goal-setting plans for both a small and large church.

For a small church, beginning with four D-Groups and a 40 to 50 percent DMR is a realistic starting point. In the chart below, let's look at a ten-year goal-setting plan for a church starting with four D-Groups and a 40 percent DMR.

## Church Starting with 4 D-Groups / 10-Year Growth Goals with a 40% DMR

|  | Discipleship Groups (Grow in Spiritual Maturity) | Ministry Projects (Serve in Missional Ministry) | New Leaders (Reproduce Disciple Makers) |
|---|---|---|---|
| Year 1 | 4 | 24 | 2 |
| Year 2 | 6 | 36 | 2 |
| Year 3 | 8 | 48 | 3 |
| Year 4 | 11 | 66 | 4 |
| Year 5 | 15 | 90 | 6 |
| Year 6 | 21 | 126 | 8 |
| Year 7 | 29 | 174 | 12 |
| Year 8 | 41 | 432 | 16 |
| Year 9 | 57 | 342 | 23 |
| Year 10 | 80 | 480 | 32 |

In the first column, the ten-year growth in the number of D-Groups expands from 4 to 80 groups. If you average 5 people in each group, you will go from 20 to 400 people participating in a D-Group where they are certain to grow in spiritual maturity.

In the second column, you see the ten-year growth in the number of ministry projects your groups will do outside the walls of the church. If each D-Group does 6 ministry projects a year—as they are trained to do—you will go from 24 to 480 projects as your people serve in missional ministry. Imagine the impact this will have on the community.

In the third column is the ten-year growth in new D-Group leaders from 2 to 32. Each year you are equipping new leaders to reproduce as disciple-makers.

This is the power of spiritual fission. It produces growth without gimmicks. For a small church, you will experience spiritual and physical growth that is healthy and sustainable. This is the result of building a disciple-making culture for church revitalization.

Now, let's consider the same plan for a larger church. For a large church, beginning with 30 D-Groups and a 30 to 40 percent DMR is a realistic starting point. In the chart below, let's look at a ten-year goal-setting plan for a church starting with 30 D-Groups and a 33.3 percent DMR.

## Church Starting with 30 D-Groups / 10-Year Growth Goals with a 33.3% DMR

| | Discipleship Groups (Grow in Spiritual Maturity) | Ministry Projects (Serve in Missional Ministry) | New Leaders (Reproduce Disciple Makers) |
|---|---|---|---|
| Year 1 | 30 | 180 | 10 |
| Year 2 | 40 | 240 | 13 |
| Year 3 | 53 | 318 | 18 |
| Year 4 | 71 | 426 | 24 |
| Year 5 | 95 | 570 | 32 |
| Year 6 | 127 | 762 | 42 |
| Year 7 | 169 | 1014 | 56 |
| Year 8 | 225 | 1350 | 75 |
| Year 9 | 300 | 1800 | 100 |
| Year 10 | 400 | 2400 | 128 |

In the first column, the ten-year growth in the number of D-Groups is from 30 to 400 groups. If you average 5 people in each group, you will go from 150 to 2,000 people participating in a D-Group where they are certain to grow in spiritual maturity.

In the second column, is the ten-year growth in the number of ministry projects your groups will do outside the walls of the church. If each D-Group does 6 ministry projects a year—as they are trained to do—you will go from 180 to 2,400 projects as your people serve in missional ministry. Again, imagine the impact this will have on your community.

In the third column, you see growth in new D-Group leaders from 10 to 128. Each year you are equipping new leaders to reproduce as disciple-makers.

Wow! This is healthy growth. By building a disciple-making culture, church revitalization will come in the form of both spiritual and physical growth regardless of your size or location.

You can use a similar chart to determine your own goals for your church. Once you know how many D-Groups you can start with and the rate you expect them to multiply (DMR), you are ready to set your ten-year disciple-making goals. This will give you the metrics to come back later and set goals for other ministries. You want your disciple-making goals to complement all your ministries and to supply them with energy and power for growth.

Be sure to track your goals and work hard to achieve them. Bring D-Group leaders together at least three times a year for celebration and accountability. Share testimonies of spiritual growth, tell stories of missional ministry, and celebrate the birth of new groups. Above all, give all the glory to Him who said, "Not by might, nor by power, but by my Spirit, says the LORD of hosts" (Zechariah 4:6).

## Some Final Thoughts

A well-known pastor of a popular megachurch talks about "catching spiritual waves" as a key to church growth. However, what if church growth was never meant to be that subjective? What if it was really about the objective hard work of living out the Great Commission? I believe it is.

Jesus never talked about catching a spiritual wave but about doing a greater work. Are you tired of waiting on a wave to catch? Let's make our own waves by joining with Jesus in the greater work of making disciples who make disciples.

If I can assist in working through your plan for revitalization or in providing training for your leaders, please contact me.

## Discussion Questions for a Small Group Study

1. Why is church revitalization an important issue in the world today? In what ways would you describe your own church's need for revitalization? To experience revitalization in your church, why is it vital to build a disciple-making culture? How would you define a true disciple-making culture?

2. What is the "Aaron's calf" approach to discipleship? How is this approach different from what Jesus taught us to do? Do you have any programs in your church that have become a golden calf? If so, what should you do about this? Why do you think some people love the programs of the church more than the mission of the church?

3. According to the author, what are the five steps to building a disciple-making culture for church revitalization? Why must it begin with prayer? Why does building a disciple-making culture require a disciple-making pastor? What steps can you take to unify your leadership around the vision to build a disciple-making culture?

4. What is a true disciple-making process? In what ways is this a missing link for many churches? From Jesus' example, what is the three-fold purpose of a D-Group? How did Jesus show "strategic intentionality" in disciple-making? Does your church have anything that resembles the relationship between Jesus and his disciples?

5. Why is the illustration of an atom a good way to rethink your church's model for ministry? What is a D-Group Multiplication Rate (DMR), and how can this help you develop smart disciple-making goals? What is "spiritual fission"? How can spiritual fission help you to build a disciple-making culture for church revitalization?

**Closing Prayer:** Heavenly Father, we pray for a powerful movement of your Holy Spirit in our church as we seek to build a disciple-making culture for church revitalization.

# CHAPTER 12

# Follow the Leader

*So Peter got out of the boat and walked on the water and came to Jesus.
But when he saw the wind, he was afraid, and beginning to sink he cried
out, "Lord, save me."*
—Matthew 14:29–30

Do you remember playing "Follow the Leader" when you were a child? For some reason, it was always fun to imitate the actions of the one in front. The challenge of the game was to follow a bold leader who was willing to do bold things.

Likewise, today's church needs bold leaders who are willing to do bold things. Church revitalization will not come easy. It will require courageous leadership and a congregation that is willing to follow the leader.

As a disciple of Jesus, there were times when Peter attempted to be a bold leader. In Matthew 14, we read the story of Peter walking on water. As a bold leader, Peter was willing to step out of a storm-tossed boat and walk on water to Jesus. But when he felt the wind and saw the splashing water, he was afraid and began to sink. When he cried out for help, Jesus reached out and lifted him from the water.

As we discussed this story in a D-Group I was leading, one of the men in our group made an interesting observation. He said that the most important person in the story could have been the second man out of the boat. This insight piqued my interest. I had never thought about this before.

He went on to explain that every leader needs a second man. If you are at an event where one man begins to clap, he looks foolish. But, if a second person starts clapping with him, then the rest of the crowd will begin to clap. Likewise, if one man stands up alone, he looks foolish. But, if a second person stands with him, then the rest of the crowd is likely to stand.

Peter needed a second man. If a second man had stepped out of the boat, it's likely the others would have walked on water with Jesus, and Peter would have never started to sink. This is the power of the second man.

## The Significance of the Second Man

No church has to sink. I believe revitalization can come to every church that is willing to build a disciple-making culture. However, it will require a bold leader and a second man.

If your church has a bold leader with a vision to do bold things for God, you are greatly blessed. But no leader can do it alone. There must be a second man. When other key people join in the vision, the rest of the church is likely to follow the leader.

In the church, everything rises or falls on leadership. Follow your leader in doing the greater work and your church can experience a great revival.

## The Importance of the Greater Work

Nehemiah was a bold leader for God. The enemy had destroyed the city of Jerusalem and torn down its protective walls. God gave Nehemiah a vision to revitalize the Holy City and to rebuild her walls.

After much prayer and fasting, Nehemiah set out on his noble quest. Upon his arrival in Jerusalem, he surveyed the situation, developed a plan, and shared the vision with the people. The hand of God was upon him when he said to the people, "Let us rise up and build" (Nehemiah 2:18).

At first, everything went well. The people came to work, and the walls were going up. However, some in the city didn't agree with the vision. They had become satisfied with things as they were and had no desire to work.

Sanballat and Tobiah were two prominent leaders who became angry. They plotted against Nehemiah and the work he was doing. In every conceivable way, they tried to stop the people from working and to get Nehemiah to come down off the wall he was building.

I love Nehemiah's response to Sanballat and Tobiah. With great conviction in his heart, he boldly said, "I am doing a great work and I cannot come down" (Nehemiah 6:3). Because of Nehemiah's strong conviction and devotion to the great work that he was doing, the walls around Jerusalem were rebuilt in record time.

As a bold leader, Nehemiah is a great example to follow. When God gives you the vision to build a disciple-making culture in your church, you can be certain that it's a noble quest. After praying it through, survey the situation, develop a plan, and share the vision with your people. The hand of God will be on you when you say to your people, "Let us rise up and build."

Trust the Lord to give you a second man and others who will follow your lead. However, don't be naïve or caught off guard. There will likely be a few Sanballats and Tobiahs in the crowd. No matter how noble the vision, there will be those who have no desire for the greater work. It can be tempting to become discouraged and to throw in the towel. Don't do it! Too much is at stake.

Do your job! Building a disciple-making movement in your church is the most important thing you can ever do. God will be with you and He will help you do it. When a Sanballat or Tobiah tells you that you can't—never lose sight of your vision. Recall the words of another great leader and say to your distractors, "I'm doing a great work and I cannot come down!" You're not just doing a great work, you're doing *THE GREATER WORK*. Don't give up. Don't ever give up.

## 🔍 Discussion Questions for a Small Group Study

1. What is the significance of the second man when it comes to following the leader? When Peter walked on water to Jesus, what do you think would have happened if a second man had stepped out of the boat? Why does every bold leader need a second man?

2. Do you believe that revitalization can come to every church that is willing to build a disciple-making culture? Why or why not? Who was Nehemiah and in what ways did he demonstrate the qualities of a bold leader for God? What did God give Nehemiah a vision to do?

3. Who were Sanballat and Tobiah? Why were these two men opposed to the great work that Nehemiah had set out to do? When they tried to get Nehemiah to come down from the wall he was building, what great answer did he give them? Why must a bold leader never be caught off guard by Sanballats and Tobiahs?

4. Why is building a disciple-making movement in your church the most important thing you can do? No matter the obstacles, why must you never give up on this noble vision? How can you be certain that God will be with you when you are doing the greater work?

5. What is the most important thing that you will take away from the reading of this book? Will you choose to be the "second man" and support your church's vision to building a disciple-making culture for revitalization? Will you commit your life to the greater work of making disciples who make disciples? Why would you not?

**Closing Prayer:** Heavenly Father, give us faith and courage as we begin to live a lifestyle of disciple-making and to build a disciple-making culture in our church.

# APPENDIX 1

# D-Life Journal Sample Materials

# INTRODUCTION

Jesus charged His disciples with making disciples (Matthew 28:19), baptizing in His name and teaching them His commandments. That charge is just as relevant today as it was to the first-century church. Becoming a disciple is more than being saved and baptized. Becoming a disciple involves learning to follow God by carefully and diligently studying God's Word and then by intentionally living God's Word for others to see.

Discipleship is a journey and life-long process. It involves daily seeking to know God's heart, studying God's Word, and then living out God's expectations. It is not an easy journey, but it is more rewarding than any other endeavor in this life.

*D-Life Journal* is a discipleship tool that can be used as a guide for personal spiritual growth or in a discipleship group. Groups can begin with as few as three to five members. New groups should be started when a group enrollment reaches eight. To begin a discipleship group, consider creating diversity within the group, such as:

- New believers, who can benefit by connecting in discipleship to other believers.

- Unbelievers and the unchurched who are open to hearing about Jesus.

- Multi-generational believers, who bring different life stages and different spiritual journeys into the group.

- Believers struggling in life with issues such as drug abuse, depression, and gender identification, who will benefit from having the support and accountability of other believers.

## HOW TO LEAD A D-LIFE GROUP:

- **Fellowship Time** – Create fellowship within the group wherever it meets—a coffee shop, café, home, park, school, or church. Share coffee, a snack, or a meal.

- **Accountability Time** – Create accountability each week by asking if group members read their Bibles daily. Lead them to share some application points written in their notes.

- **Prayer Time**– Develop an on-going emphasis on prayer, with members taking responsibility for leading the group in prayer, praying for specific prayer requests, and praying for revival in our land.

- **Tell the Story** – Assign a member in the group each week to tell the biblical story or paraphrase the passage to be studied in his or her own words.

- **Read the Story** – Assign another member in the group to read the passage to be studied from the Bible. See if anything was left out of the storytelling.

- **Facilitate Bible Study** – Assign another member in your group to facilitate the Bible study using the questions provided in the weekly study guide.

  When facilitating, use the study guide questions with intention. When time is an issue, use only 3 to 5 questions and work to intentionally involve all group members in discussion. Keep the discussion on point. Be truthful, positive, and transparent. Clearly address theological issues when necessary. Be sensitive to the Holy Spirit.

- **Ministry Planning Time** – Spend a few minutes planning for your next ministry project. You will do one ministry and evangelism project every two months.

- **Weekly Assignments** –Assign tasks for the next week to different members of the group: lead in prayer, tell the story, read the story, and facilitate the Bible study.

# S-P-A-C-E BIBLE STUDY METHOD

A major goal of D-Life is to lead people to develop a life long habit of daily Bible reading. This alone is life changing. Each day we want to make SPACE in our hearts for God's Word by writing down one personal application point from our daily Bible reading assignments. We make **S-P-A-C-E** by asking five simple questions as we read each chapter. Ask, is there a:

- **S**in to confess?
- **P**romise to claim?
- **A**ttitude to change?
- **C**ommand to obey?
- **E**xample to follow?

In each chapter you will find an answer to at least one of these question. Ask God to give you a personal word as you read. Let the Holy Spirit speak to your heart. As you ask these questions, let God show you a personal point of application. Psalm 119:18 is a great prayer to pray, "Open my eyes, that I may behold wondrous things out of your law."

When God speaks to your heart, you want to write it down. In your journal, circle the appropriate letter in the acrostic **S-P-A-C-E** that relates to your application point and write a brief note reflecting your thoughts. For example, in John 3:16, you may see a "Promise to claim." Circle the letter "P" and then you may write something like: "What a great promise to claim! God loves me and has given me eternal life through faith in His Son. Thank you God for your incredible gift to me."

It's helpful to have a certain time and place where you meet alone with God each day for prayer and Bible reading. Make your daily time alone with God a major priority in your life.

# THE MINISTRY OF D-LIFE

To make disciples like Jesus, we must personally train our disciples to do the work of ministry and evangelism "outside the walls" of the church. This is an important part of living the D-Life.

Therefore, every D-Group must be committed to do the work of ministry and evangelism. We cannot disciple others through fellowship and Bible study alone. We MUST be willing to go outside the walls of the church and share in the work of ministry and evangelism together.

**THE MINIMUM GOAL OF EVERY D-GROUP** is to work together on **one** community ministry and evangelism project every **two** months. This means that every D-Group will participate in a minimum of **six** ministry projects each year. This is a reasonable expectation and an absolute essential for making genuine disciples.

Planning for ministry projects should be a regular part of weekly D-Group meetings. We should keep notes about ministry ideas and upcoming projects. Ministry Projects may include things such as feeding the homeless, crashing someone's yard for lawn care, doing a work project at a local school, building a wheelchair ramp, adopting a family for Christmas, prayer walk evangelism, or other creative ideas. The opportunities are endless. D-Groups can even make plans to go on a mission trip together.

The purpose for all D-Group ministry projects is servant evangelism. We want to advance God's Kingdom on earth.

Kyle Martin, with *TIME TO REVIVE* (www.timetorevive.com), teaches a simple and effective approach to servant evangelism involving the following four steps...

- **Love** – Approach an individual and engage in friendly conversation. Our main concern is to show them love. Then ask, *"Is there anything we can pray for you about?"*
- **Listen** – Listen carefully to him or her and show genuine concern.
- **Discern** – Spiritually discern how you should respond to each individual.
- **Respond** – When appropriate, pray with the individual and share the Gospel.

The *TIME TO REVIVE BIBLE* published by LIFE BIBLE STUDY (www.lifebiblestudy.com) is an excellent tool to use for sharing the Gospel. You can also use THE GOSPEL presentation on your D-Life Web App. Simply turn your mobile phone landscape and flip through the Bible verses as you present the Gospel.

## USE THE SPACE BELOW TO PLAN AND KEEP A JOURNAL OF YOUR PROJECTS:

### D-GROUP MINISTRY PROJECT #1
Date of Project: _____
Journal Notes on Project: _____
_____
_____
_____

### D-GROUP MINISTRY PROJECT #2
Date of Project: _____
Journal Notes on Project: _____
_____
_____
_____

### D-GROUP MINISTRY PROJECT #3
Date of Project: _____

Journal Notes on Project: _____

_____

_____

_____

### D-GROUP MINISTRY PROJECT #4
Date of Project: _____

Journal Notes on Project: _____

_____

_____

_____

### D-GROUP MINISTRY PROJECT #5
Date of Project: _____

Journal Notes on Project: _____

_____

_____

_____

### D-GROUP MINISTRY PROJECT #6
Date of Project: _____

Journal Notes on Project: _____

_____

_____

_____

# D-LIFE SCRIPTURE MEMORY

*Your word I have hidden in my heart, that I might not sin against You (Psalm 119:11).*

### Why Memorize the Scripture

Scripture memory is an important spiritual discipline for a disciple of Christ. The Psalmist said, "Your word I have hidden in my heart, that I might not sin against You" (Psalm 119:11). Jesus memorized the Scripture. He quoted often from the Old Testament in His teaching and used Scripture to ward off the temptation of Satan in the wilderness. The early apostles memorized the Scripture and quoted it often as they witnessed to others and as they defended their faith. By memorizing the Scripture, you will have a valuable tool in hand to assist you in witnessing, counseling, or resisting the temptation of the enemy.

### How to Memorize the Scripture

You will want to memorize the Scripture from the Bible translation that you normally use for your Bible reading. Write out the weekly memory verse(s) on an index card or small sheet of paper. Keep the handwritten copy of the verse(s) with you and review it when you are getting dressed in the morning, riding to work, and at night before you go to bed. Go over it several times a day committing each part of the verse(s) to memory. Strive to memorize the verse(s) word-for-word and always give the chapter and verse reference. Say the verse(s) out load to yourself and be prepared to share it at your weekly D-Group meeting. You will also want to review the verse(s) for at least three more weeks to fully commit it to memory. If you don't review it, you will lose it.

### The D-Life Plan for Memorizing Scripture

In D-Life, you will memorize selected Scriptures that come out of your weekly Bible reading plan. You will have weekly memory verses for all 52 weeks of the year. These verses will come from many different books of the Bible. Scripture memory is an optional part of leading a D-Group, but it is highly recommended and encouraged. Whether or not to use Scripture memory in your D-Group will depend on the commitment level of your group and your goals as a leader.

*Your word is a lamp to my feet and a light to my path (Psalm 119:105).*

## WEEKLY MEMORY VERSES FOR NEW TESTAMENT 1
Memorize each verse in 1 week and review it for 3 weeks (check it off as you go)...

Review

Wk 01: ☐ ☐ ☐ ☐ Matthew 4:19
Wk 02: ☐ ☐ ☐ ☐ Matthew 7:7
Wk 03: ☐ ☐ ☐ ☐ Matthew 11:28-30
Wk 04: ☐ ☐ ☐ ☐ Matthew 18:19-20
Wk 05: ☐ ☐ ☐ ☐ Matthew 22:37-39
Wk 06: ☐ ☐ ☐ ☐ Matthew 28:18-20
Wk 07: ☐ ☐ ☐ ☐ Mark 3:14-15
Wk 08: ☐ ☐ ☐ ☐ Mark 8:36-37
Wk 09: ☐ ☐ ☐ ☐ Mark 14:38
Wk 10: ☐ ☐ ☐ ☐ Luke 5:31-32
Wk 11: ☐ ☐ ☐ ☐ Luke 9:23
Wk 12: ☐ ☐ ☐ ☐ Luke 12:15
Wk 13: ☐ ☐ ☐ ☐ Luke 18:16-17
Wk 14: ☐ ☐ ☐ ☐ Luke 24:46-47
Wk 15: ☐ ☐ ☐ ☐ John 3:16
Wk 16: ☐ ☐ ☐ ☐ John 8:31-32
Wk 17: ☐ ☐ ☐ ☐ John 13:34-35
Wk 18: ☐ ☐ ☐ ☐ John 20:31
Wk 19: ☐ ☐ ☐ ☐ Acts 2:38
Wk 20: ☐ ☐ ☐ ☐ Acts 10:34-35
Wk 21: ☐ ☐ ☐ ☐ Acts 13:38-39
Wk 22: ☐ ☐ ☐ ☐ Acts 17:30-31
Wk 23: ☐ ☐ ☐ ☐ Acts 22:16
Wk 24: ☐ ☐ ☐ ☐ Romans 1:16
Wk 25: ☐ ☐ ☐ ☐ Romans 5:8
Wk 26: ☐ ☐ ☐ ☐ Romans 10:9-10

Review

Wk 27: ☐ ☐ ☐ ☐ Romans 15:1
Wk 28: ☐ ☐ ☐ ☐ 1 Corinthians 4:1-2
Wk 29: ☐ ☐ ☐ ☐ 1 Corinthians 9:22
Wk 30: ☐ ☐ ☐ ☐ 1 Corinthians 13:13
Wk 31: ☐ ☐ ☐ ☐ 2 Corinthians 5:17
Wk 32: ☐ ☐ ☐ ☐ 2 Corinthians 8:9
Wk 33: ☐ ☐ ☐ ☐ Galatians 2:20
Wk 34: ☐ ☐ ☐ ☐ Galatians 5:16
Wk 35: ☐ ☐ ☐ ☐ Ephesians 6:10-11
Wk 36: ☐ ☐ ☐ ☐ Philippians 2:3-4
Wk 37: ☐ ☐ ☐ ☐ Colossians 3:2
Wk 38: ☐ ☐ ☐ ☐ 1 Thessalonians 4:3-4
Wk 39: ☐ ☐ ☐ ☐ 1 Timothy 1:15
Wk 40: ☐ ☐ ☐ ☐ 2 Timothy 2:1-2
Wk 41: ☐ ☐ ☐ ☐ Titus 2:11-12
Wk 42: ☐ ☐ ☐ ☐ Hebrews 4:12
Wk 43: ☐ ☐ ☐ ☐ Hebrews 7:25
Wk 44: ☐ ☐ ☐ ☐ Hebrews 12:1
Wk 45: ☐ ☐ ☐ ☐ James 4:7-8
Wk 46: ☐ ☐ ☐ ☐ 1 Peter 5:6-7
Wk 47: ☐ ☐ ☐ ☐ 1 John 3:17-18
Wk 48: ☐ ☐ ☐ ☐ 3 John 1:4
Wk 49: ☐ ☐ ☐ ☐ Revelation 3:15
Wk 50: ☐ ☐ ☐ ☐ Revelation 11:15
Wk 51: ☐ ☐ ☐ ☐ Revelation 15:4
Wk 52: ☐ ☐ ☐ ☐ Revelation 22:7

### Instructions for D-Life Scripture Memory

• Memorize the verse(s) from the Bible translation you normally use.
• Write out the verse(s) on an index card or small sheet of paper.
• Review the verse(s) several times a day as you dress, ride to work, and go to bed.
• Commit each part of the verse(s) to memory throughout the week.
• Strive to memorize the verse(s) word-for-word and always give the reference.
• Say the verse(s) out load to yourself before your D-Group meeting.
• Be prepared to share the verse(s) at your weekly D-Group meeting.
• Review the verse(s) for at least three more weeks to fully commit it to memory.

# WEEK

**Weekly Bible Reading:** ................................. Matthew 1-5
**Weekly Bible Study:** ............................... Matthew 4:18-25

## MATTHEW 1                    [CIRCLE ONE: S P A C E ]
*Personal Study Notes:* _____
_____
_____
_____

## MATTHEW 2                    [CIRCLE ONE: S P A C E ]
*Personal Study Notes:* _____
_____
_____
_____

## MATTHEW 3                    [CIRCLE ONE: S P A C E ]
*Personal Study Notes:* _____
_____
_____
_____

## MATTHEW 4                    [CIRCLE ONE: S P A C E ]
*Personal Study Notes:* _____
_____
_____
_____

## MATTHEW 5                    [CIRCLE ONE: S P A C E ]
*Personal Study Notes:* _____
_____
_____
_____

Read carefully one chapter of the Bible five days a week. In each chapter look for a . . .
**S**in to Confess / **P**romise to Claim / **A**ttitude to Change / **C**ommand to Obey / **E**xample to Follow.

# FISHING FOR MEN
### (MATTHEW 4:18-25)

## WEEKLY ASSIGNMENTS:

Lead Prayer Time: _____

Tell the Story (Paraphrase): _____

Read the Text: _____

Facilitate Bible Study: _____

## DISCUSSION QUESTIONS:

- If someone wanted to go fishing today, what different tools or equipment would he or she need to take in order to catch some fish? How hard would it be to catch fish without these tools?

- In our story, Jesus is fishing for some men to be His first disciples. Who were these men and what fishing tools did they leave behind to follow Jesus? What kind of tools would Jesus begin to teach them to use to fish for people?

- Jesus said to them, "Follow me, and I will make you fishers of men" (v. 19). What do you think Jesus meant by this command? As a command for us to obey, in what ways should we be fishing for people today to become new followers of Jesus? What kind of tools can help us with this?

- Read Matt. 28:18-20. How does Jesus' first command to His followers found here in Matt. 4:19 compare to His final command in the Great Commission? In these two commands, what is Jesus saying about our purpose in life?

- As Jesus and His first disciples went throughout Galilee, what things did they observe Him doing (v. 23-24)? By proclaiming the gospel and caring for the afflicted, how was Jesus training His new followers to be "fishers of men?"

- What is the "gospel of the kingdom" (v.23) that Jesus preached? Can someone share about the time when you opened your heart to the gospel?

- As Jesus taught and cared for the people, "His fame spread" in Syria (v.24). In what ways are you helping make Jesus famous in the world today?

- As we join together in our D-Group, how will this help you become a stronger follower of Christ? How can D-Life be a tool that helps you fish for others?

## PRAYER:

Let's pray today that each of us will grow stronger in our faith and better at fishing for new followers of Christ as we join together in D-Life.

**PRAYER REQUESTS:**

**BI-MONTHLY MISSION PROJECT NOTES:**

# WEEK ②

**Weekly Bible Reading:** ................................. Matthew 6-10
**Weekly Bible Study:** ................................ Matthew 6:5-13

## MATTHEW 6
[CIRCLE ONE: S P A C E ]

*Personal Study Notes:* _____
_____
_____
_____

## MATTHEW 7
[CIRCLE ONE: S P A C E ]

*Personal Study Notes:* _____
_____
_____
_____

## MATTHEW 8
[CIRCLE ONE: S P A C E ]

*Personal Study Notes:* _____
_____
_____
_____

## MATTHEW 9
[CIRCLE ONE: S P A C E ]

*Personal Study Notes:* _____
_____
_____
_____

## MATTHEW 10
[CIRCLE ONE: S P A C E ]

*Personal Study Notes:* _____
_____
_____
_____

Read carefully one chapter of the Bible five days a week. In each chapter look for a . . .
**S**in to Confess / **P**romise to Claim / **A**ttitude to Change / **C**ommand to Obey / **E**xample to Follow.

# THE LORD'S PRAYER
### (MATTHEW 6:5-13)

## WEEKLY ASSIGNMENTS:

Lead Prayer Time: _____

Tell the Story (Paraphrase): _____

Read the Text: _____

Facilitate Bible Study: _____

## DISCUSSION QUESTIONS:

- Can someone give a testimony of a time when God answered your prayer? Why is it important for us to pray?

- In our story, Jesus taught about prayer. How many times did He say, "When you pray?" Why do you think He said, "When you pray," instead of, "If you pray?"

- Where did Jesus say that "the hypocrites" liked to pray and what was their motive? What did Jesus say about their reward? What is a hypocrite?

- Where did Jesus say we should go to pray? When we do this, what did Jesus say the Father would do? Do you have a special place where you like to pray?

- Do you think it's important to pray every day? Why or why not? How much time should we spend in prayer? When is the best time for you to pray?

- Why should we not repeat meaningless phrases when we pray? Why must we pray sincere prayers from the heart instead of elegant prayers to impress others?

- What did Jesus say the Father knows about our needs even before we ask? Why is it still important for us to pray about our needs?

- In Jesus' model prayer, there is praise, intercession, petition, and confession. This is *an example to follow*. When we pray, why is it important to spend some time giving thanks and praise to God? Why should we confess our sins to God? Why should we intercede for others? Why is it important for us to pray for ourselves?

- Like daily Bible reading, prayer is a vital spiritual discipline. What did you learn from this study that can help you have a more consistent and faithful prayer life?

## PRAYER:

Let's pray for one another today to be faithful in the daily spiritual discipline of prayer.

**WEEK 2**

## PRAYER REQUESTS:

## BI-MONTHLY MISSION PROJECT NOTES:

# APPENDIX 2

# D-Life Online Sample Materials

# dlife

## D-Life Bible Study

**Weekly Bible Reading:**     **Matthew 1-5**
**Weekly Bible Study:**       **Matthew 4:18-25**

### Matthew 1
[Circle One: S P A C E ]
☐ Personal Study Notes:_____
_____
_____
_____

### Matthew 2
[Circle One: S P A C E ]
☐ Personal Study Notes:_____
_____
_____
_____

### Matthew 3
[Circle One: S P A C E ]
☐ Personal Study Notes:_____
_____
_____
_____

### Matthew 4
[Circle One: S P A C E ]
☐ Personal Study Notes:_____
_____
_____
_____

### Matthew 5
[Circle One: S P A C E ]
☐ Personal Study Notes:_____
_____
_____
_____

Read carefully one chapter of the Bible five days a week. In each chapter look for a . . .
**S**in to Confess / **P**romise to Claim / **A**ttitude to Change / **C**ommand to Obey / **E**xample to Follow.

## *Fishing for People* (Matthew 4:18-25)

**Weekly Assignments:**

- *Lead Prayer Time:* _____
- *Tell the Story (Paraphrase):* _____
- *Read the Text:* _____
- *Facilitate Bible Study:* _____

**Discussion Questions:**

- If someone wanted to go fishing today, what different tools or equipment would he or she need to take in order to catch some fish? How hard would it be to catch fish without these tools?

- In our story, Jesus goes fishing for some men to be His first disciples. Who were these men and what fishing tools did they leave behind to follow Jesus? What kind of tools would Jesus begin to teach them to use to fish for people?

- Jesus said to them, "Follow me, and I will make you fishers of men" (v. 19). What do you think Jesus meant by this command? As a *command for us to obey,* in what ways should we be fishing for people today to become new followers of Jesus? What kind of tools can help us with this?

- Read Matt. 28:18-20. How does Jesus' first command to His followers found here in Matt. 4:19 compare to His final command in the Great Commission? In these two commands, what is Jesus saying about our purpose in life?

- As Jesus and His first disciples went throughout Galilee, what things did they observe Him doing (v. 23-24)? By proclaiming the gospel and caring for the afflicted, how was Jesus training His new followers to be "fishers of men?"

- What is the "gospel of the kingdom" (v. 23) that Jesus preached? Can someone share about the time when you opened your heart to the gospel?

- As Jesus taught and cared for the people, "His fame spread" in Syria (v. 24). In what ways are you helping make Jesus famous in the world today?

- As we join together in our D-Group, how will this help you become a stronger follower of Christ? How can D-Life be a tool that helps you fish for others?

**Prayer:** Let's pray today that each of us will grow stronger in our faith and better at fishing for new followers of Christ as we join together in D-Life.

**Prayer Requests:**

**Bi-Monthly Mission Project Notes:**

# dlife

## D-Life Bible Study

**Weekly Bible Reading:**   Matthew 6-10
**Weekly Bible Study:**   Matthew 6:5-13

### Matthew 6
[Circle One: S P A C E ]
☐ Personal Study Notes:_____
_____
_____
_____

### Matthew 7
[Circle One: S P A C E ]
☐ Personal Study Notes:_____
_____
_____
_____

### Matthew 8
[Circle One: S P A C E ]
☐ Personal Study Notes:_____
_____
_____
_____

### Matthew 9
[Circle One: S P A C E ]
☐ Personal Study Notes:_____
_____
_____
_____

### Matthew 10
[Circle One: S P A C E ]
☐ Personal Study Notes:_____
_____
_____
_____

Read carefully one chapter of the New Testament five days a week. In each chapter look for a . . .
Sin to Confess / Promise to Claim / Attitude to Change / Command to Obey / Example to Follow.

## *The Lord's Prayer* (Matthew 6:5-13)

**Weekly Assignments:**

- *Lead Prayer Time:* _____
- *Tell the Story (Paraphrase):* _____
- *Read the Text:* _____
- *Facilitate Bible Study:* _____

**Discussion Questions:**

- Can someone give a testimony of a time when God answered your prayer? Why is it important for us to pray?

- In our story, Jesus taught about prayer. How many times did He say, "When you pray?" Why do you think He said, "When you pray," instead of, "If you pray?"

- Where did Jesus say that "the hypocrites" liked to pray and what was their motive? What did Jesus say about their reward? What is a hypocrite?

- Where did Jesus say we should go to pray? When we do this, what did Jesus say the Father would do? Do you have a special place where you like to pray?

- Do you think it's important to pray every day? Why or why not? How much time should we spend in prayer? When is the best time for you to pray?

- Why should we not repeat meaningless phrases when we pray? Why must we pray sincere prayers from the heart instead of elegant prayers to impress others?

- What did Jesus say the Father knows about our needs even before we ask? Why is it still important for us to pray about our needs?

- In Jesus' model prayer, there is praise, intercession, petition, and confession. This is *an example to follow.* When we pray, why is it important to spend some time giving thanks and praise to God? Why should we confess our sins to God? Why should we intercede for others? Why is it important for us to pray for ourselves?

- Like daily Bible reading, prayer is a vital spiritual discipline. What did you learn from this study that can help you have a more consistent and faithful prayer life?

**Prayer:** Let's pray for one another today to be faithful in the daily spiritual discipline of prayer.

**Prayer Requests:**

**Bi-Monthly Mission Project Notes:**

# dlife

*D-Life Bible Study*

**Weekly Bible Reading:** Matthew 11-15
**Weekly Bible Study:** Matthew 13:3-9, 18-23

## Matthew 11
[Circle One: S P A C E ]
☐ Personal Study Notes:_____
_____
_____
_____

## Matthew 12
[Circle One: S P A C E ]
☐ Personal Study Notes:_____
_____
_____
_____

## Matthew 13
[Circle One: S P A C E ]
☐ Personal Study Notes:_____
_____
_____
_____

## Matthew 14
[Circle One: S P A C E ]
☐ Personal Study Notes:_____
_____
_____
_____

## Matthew 15
[Circle One: S P A C E ]
☐ Personal Study Notes:_____
_____
_____
_____

Read carefully one chapter of the New Testament five days a week. In each chapter look for a . . .
**S**in to Confess / **P**romise to Claim / **A**ttitude to Change / **C**ommand to Obey / **E**xample to Follow.

## *The Sower and the Seed* (Matthew 13:3-9, 18-23)

**Weekly Assignments:**

- *Lead Prayer Time:* _____
- *Tell the Story (Paraphrase):* _____
- *Read the Text:* _____
- *Facilitate Bible Study:* _____

**Discussion Questions:**

- o  Have you ever tried to grow anything? If so, what did you try to grow and how are your gardening skills? What have you learned about gardening?

- o  In our story, Jesus told a story about gardening and explained its meaning. Who did "the sower" represent and what is "the seed" that he was sowing? What did the different types of soil represent?

- o  Who did the birds represent and what did they do to the seeds that fell by the wayside? In what ways does "the evil one" snatch away the Gospel seed?

- o  Why do you think some people develop a hard heart toward God and the good news of the Gospel? What are the best ways to share our faith with people who are hardened toward God and the Gospel?

- o  What did the rocky soil represent? What two things did Jesus say reveal a shallow commitment to Christ? What happens to the seed in this soil?

- o  What did the thorny soil represent? What two things did Jesus say reveal an uncertain commitment to Christ? What happens to the seed in this soil?

- o  What did the good soil represent? What is the one thing that reveals a true commitment to Christ? What is spiritual fruit? Do all true believers bear spiritual fruit? Why do you think some believers bear more fruit than others?

- o  In what way is the sower *an example to follow*? Even though everyone will not be receptive, why is it important for us to continually share our faith?

- o  Which of the soils in this story do you most identify with and why? In what ways can your life become more fruitful for God?

**Prayer:** Let's pray for one another today that our lives will bear much fruit for God.

**Prayer Requests:**

**Bi-Monthly Mission Project Notes:**

# Notes

1   James Emery White, *The Rise of the Nones: Understanding and Reaching the Religiously Unaffiliated*, (Grand Rapids: Baker Books, 2014), 18.

2   Kate Shellnutt, "Southern Baptists Down to Lowest in 30 Years," *Christianity Today*, May 23, 2019, https://www.christianitytoday.com/news/2019/may/southern-baptists-acp-membership-baptism-decline-2018.html.

3   Shellnutt.

4   Tom Strode, "SBC Panel on Sexual Abuse Calls for Action," Lifeway Research, June 11, 2019, https://lifewayresearch.com/2019/06/11/sbc-panel-on-sexual-abuse-calls-for-action/.

5   White, *Rise of the Nones*, 17.

6   White, 16.

7   White.

8   White, 17.

9   John S. Dickerson, *The Great Evangelical Recession: 6 Factors That Will Crash the American Church . . . and How to Prepare* (Grand Rapids: Baker Books, 2013), 27.

10  Dickerson.

11  Dickerson, 132–33.

12  Scott Thumma and Warren Bird, "National Survey of Megachurch Attendees," Hartford Institute for Religion and Research, cited in Dickerson, *Great Evangelical Recession*, 23–24.

13  White, *Rise of the Nones*, 75–76.

14  White, 88.

15  Dickerson, *Great Evangelical Recession*, 240.

16  David Mathis, "Hospitality and the Great Commission," Desiring God, October 2, 2012, https://www.desiringgod.org/articles/hospitality-and-the-great-commission.

17  Donald S. Whitney, *Spiritual Disciplines for the Christian Life*, rev. ed. (Colorado Springs: NavPress, 2014), 22.

18  Ronald Dunn, *Don't Just Stand There, Pray Something: The Incredible Power of Intercessory Prayer*, (Nashville: Thomas Nelson, 1992), 19.

# About the Author

Dr. Bill Wilks is the Lead Pastor of NorthPark Church in Trussville, Alabama, where he has served since 1999. He is a graduate of Southwestern Baptist Theological Seminary with a doctor of ministry degree and frequently serves as an adjunct professor at the Birmingham extension for the New Orleans Baptist Theological Seminary.

Dr. Wilks is also the author and lead trainer for D-Life: Disciple-Making. Anytime. Anywhere. He and his wife, Rondie, are passionate about disciple-making and equipping others as disciple makers. Through D-Life, they have trained thousands of believers for a lifestyle of disciple-making in churches and ministry associations across the country.

The vision of D-Life is to see a global grassroots disciple-making movement. Dr. Wilks is highly committed to seeing this vision become reality.

## If you enjoyed this book, will you consider sharing the message with others?

Let us know your thoughts. You can let the author know by visiting or sharing a photo of the cover on our social media pages or leaving a review at a retailer's site. All of it helps us get the message out!

Email: info@ironstreammedia.com

   @ironstreammedia

---

Brookstone Publishing Group, Harambee Press, Iron Stream, Iron Stream Fiction, Iron Stream Kids, and Life Bible Study are imprints of Iron Stream Media, which derives its name from Proverbs 27:17, "As iron sharpens iron, so one person sharpens another." This sharpening describes the process of discipleship, one to another. With this in mind, Iron Stream Media provides a variety of solutions for churches, ministry leaders, and nonprofits ranging from in-depth Bible study curriculum and Christian book publishing to custom publishing and consultative services.

For more information on ISM and its imprints, please visit
IronStreamMedia.com

# MORE TITLES FOR YOU

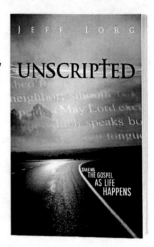